YOUR KINGDOM

Michael Perham is Dean of Derby and was an architect of *Common Worship*. He is the author of *The Sorrowful Way* and *The New Handbook of Pastoral Liturgy*, a guide to using *Common Worship* liturgies.

SIGNS OF
YOUR KINGDOM

Michael Perham

First published in Great Britain in 2002 by
Society for Promoting Christian Knowledge
Holy Trinity Church
Marylebone Road
London NW1 4DU

British Library Cataloguing-in-Publication Data
A catalogue record for this book is available
from the British Library

ISBN 0-281-05511-4

1 3 5 7 9 10 8 6 4 2

Typeset by Pioneer Associates, Perthshire
Printed in Great Britain by
Bookmarque Ltd, Croydon, Surrey

As we watch for the signs of your kingdom on earth,
we echo the song of the angels in heaven

Eucharistic Prayer F,
Common Worship

To the memory of
Edward Brooks,
Heather Openshaw
and John V. Taylor,
who in different decades of my life
nurtured my vocation
and shared with me the things of God,
with thankfulness

Contents

Preface

❧❧

Signs of Your Kingdom is about making connections. I have taken eight features of the natural world – desert, mountain, tree and garden, wheat, vine, water and oil – and explored their use in the scriptures and enjoyed finding the connections between the different passages. I have done this with the cross of Christ in the background throughout and very often coming very much into focus. What emerges is a series of seven ways into Holy Week, which I hope people might find helpful in the weeks from Ash Wednesday through till Good Friday, and a final eighth reflection for Easter Day and the new season it inaugurates. They are written with those eight weeks particularly in mind, but I hope they can be read profitably at other times too.

I have called these eight 'signs of your kingdom', echoing that striking sentence in Eucharistic Prayer F of *Common Worship* – 'we look for the signs of your kingdom on earth'. The signs of the kingdom are many and come in a variety of forms. These eight, with their sacramental quality, are only part of a much bigger picture. But, rooted as they are in scripture, I believe they can speak to us today, especially when we want to use the season of Lent preparing to enter as deeply as we can into the mystery of Christ's death and resurrection.

Three of these chapters began life, in an earlier form, as addresses in Derby Cathedral, though they have been reworked and five others added. I need to express my gratitude to that cathedral community, and to my colleagues in the clergy team there, who create an atmosphere in which it is natural to explore the mystery of faith creatively and reverently.

I record also my thanks to the staff at SPCK Publishing, especially Joanna Moriarty, who are always both helpful and encouraging.

Michael Perham
Derby
Easter Eve, 2002

ONE
Desert of Repentance

Ash Wednesday and the three days following

The first thought of the Christian as Lent begins is often of Jesus on his forty-day sojourn in the wilderness. In some ways that initial picture can lead us astray, for Lent is not much about those particular forty days. But it can be about a wilderness, desert, experience.

Two phrases from the liturgy spring to mind in relation to this experience. Neither is a direct quotation from scripture, though both have biblical echoes to them. The first is a phrase from the longer of the *Common Worship* eucharistic prefaces for Lent and it is worth quoting more fully, because it sets the scene so well.

> *In these forty days*
> *you lead us into the desert of repentance*
> *that through a pilgrimage of prayer and discipline*
> *we may grow in grace*
> *and learn to be your people once again.*
> *Through fasting, prayer and acts of service*
> *you bring us back to your generous heart.*
> *Through study of your holy word*
> *you open our eyes to your presence in the world*
> *and free our hands to welcome others*
> *into the radiant splendour of your love.*

As we prepare to celebrate the Easter feast
with joyful hearts and minds
we bless you for your mercy
and join with saints and angels.

Lent Extended Preface, *Common Worship*

The key phrase for us at this moment is 'the desert of repentance'. It is matched by another from among the *Common Worship* forms of confession:

In the wilderness we find your grace;
you love us with an everlasting love.
Lord, have mercy.

Confession 5, *Common Worship*

In a sense we cannot find God's grace till we have found the wilderness itself. It is not always far away and not altogether unfamiliar. T. S. Eliot, in his 'Choruses from the Rock', accuses the world of neglecting and belittling the desert and adds rather teasingly

The desert is not remote in southern tropics,
The desert is not only around the corner,
The desert is squeezed in the tube-train next to you,
The desert is in the heart of your brother.

Certainly in the wilderness Jesus found God's grace. Fresh from his baptism, he found himself there, with the Father's affirmation – 'You are my Son, the Beloved; with you I am well pleased' (Mark 1.11) – still ringing in his ears. Mark tells it in just two verses:

And the Spirit immediately drove him out into the wilderness. He was in the wilderness forty days, tempted by Satan; and he was with the wild beasts; and the angels waited on him.

Mark 1.12–13

Matthew and Luke both expand on Mark's economical account. It is natural to find that forty-day period highlighted in early Lent and the story of the temptations read as the gospel on the first of the Sundays of Lent. But it remains a misunderstanding to imagine that the season of Lent is about Jesus in the wilderness, in much the same way as Christmas is about the birth of Jesus or Easter about his resurrection. Lent is about preparing to celebrate what is often called 'the paschal mystery', the events from Maundy Thursday through to Easter Day and their significance for those who celebrate them. As another Lent text puts it,

You give us the spirit of discipline,
that we may triumph over evil and grow in grace,
as we prepare to celebrate the paschal mystery
with mind and heart renewed.

Lent Short Preface, Common Worship

That is the aim: to become more alert and open, so that, when Holy Week comes, we may go with Jesus through the events of that week in a way that touches us, changes us and helps us grow in love for God.

It follows that we want to use any means at our disposal to enable that to happen through the weeks

— 3 —

of Lent. One of the things that, in the providence of God, enables that to happen is an experience of the desert. That being the case, there are several stories in scripture that illustrate that experience for us. One, of course, is the experience of Jesus. In one way, it does not provide a model for us, for it tells of the sinless one, experiencing the kind of temptations that might come only to God's Son (for we do not have the powers he was determined not to abuse) and resisting the devil valiantly. That is not where we start. We are not sinless ones, we start convicted, so to speak, our temptations are different and the resolution with which we resist them less than heroic. On the other hand, it is a model in the way that it presents the desert as a good place to be, a place willingly entered, a place where we find God's grace.

Ruth Burgess, reflecting on Mark's economic account, expresses it well:

> *The desert waits,*
> *ready for those who come,*
> *who come obedient to the Spirit's leading;*
> *or who are driven,*
> *because they will not come any other way.*
> *The desert always waits,*
> *ready to let us know who we are –*
> *the place of self-discovery.*
> *And whilst we fear, and rightly,*
> *the loneliness and emptiness and harshness,*
> *we forget the angels,*
> *whom we cannot see for our blindness,*
> *but who come when God decides*

that we may need their help;
when we are ready for what they can give us.

In Janet Morley (ed.), *Bread of Tomorrow*

But there are, of course, other wilderness experiences in scripture – most of them in the Old Testament. Ishmael, Abraham's son by Hagar, is banished to the wilderness of Beersheba. David flees from Saul into the wilderness of Ziph, and Psalm 55 is written as David's cry from the desert. The psalmist wishes that he had the wings of a dove, so that he might fly away and lodge in the wilderness (Psalm 55.7). Elijah made a journey into the wilderness and sat down within it under the broom tree, with a sense of abandonment and desolation, only to encounter the Lord in 'a sound of sheer silence' (1 Kings 19.12), the 'still small voice' of the King James version of the Bible. Among the prophets, Isaiah especially speaks of the desert and it is there that John the Baptist, the prophet who links the old and new covenants, makes his home. It is into the desert that Jesus himself leads his disciples to rest awhile and it is in the desert that he feeds a great multitude.

But the Bible's great wilderness story is of the Israelite people, newly escaped from the Egyptians and with their eyes on the promised land, though sufficiently half-heartedly that they can wander for the forty years in the desert, kept there either by their own folly or divine judgement. For us the wilderness experience can be much more like theirs than like that of Jesus. For the Israelites the wilderness was both a positive and negative experience.

Yet the wilderness is being presented to us as a place where God leads us, not as a punishment, but as a good place to be – not for ever, perhaps, but for now, at least for Lent. The phrase 'the wilderness years' can be a description of a time of exile, when no one can hear you and no one wants to listen. That is how the phrase was used of Winston Churchill in the years between the two world wars of the twentieth century. For the Israelites, of course, the wilderness was both a positive and a negative experience. It was positive because it was the place of liberation, with the slavery of Pharaoh and the Egyptians left behind. It was negative because somehow they got stuck there, and it was not itself the promised land, but a series of apparently unending staging posts in hostile terrain. For the Christian the wilderness is where we find God's grace. It is God who leads us into the desert.

We are intended to pick up on the positive, to embrace the wilderness experience as a kind of escape, a sort of liberation, and to recognize it as a place not so much of staging posts as of oases, and as an experience not so much of wandering and sojourn as of journey and goal, though a bit of discomfort may not come amiss. So we are invited to enter the desert of Lent and to find it a good place to be till Easter. It is better to see it, not as a place for which we have given things up, but as a place that has allowed us to escape. For, if we have already resolved to take it seriously, by giving up this and that luxury or curtailing this or that vice, then that is only so that we can escape a slavery to the material or the physical. We leave behind that which enslaves us and so find an unexpected freedom.

So what are the marks of this wilderness experience?

The first is that the desert is a place of simplicity. For the Israelite people, the wilderness years involved leading the simple life. They had escaped from Egypt with little more than the clothes on their back, not unlike the modern refugee on our television screens. In the desert they themselves lived in tents and they even pictured Yahweh their God as living in a tent also. Their system of law was extraordinarily straight-forward and unsubtle, ten commandments for a nomadic tribe. And the food was basic – manna may have been bread from heaven, but it was hardly the Sunday roast. It is the simple life that we are bidden to recover by 'the holy fast of Lent'. That is precisely what fasting is about – going without the luxuries, so that we may recover the simple life and lose our dependence on the material. Never has that been more important than in our obscenely materialist age. So we are invited to enter the desert as a place of simplicity and rediscover even if only for a few weeks the joy of austere living.

The desert is also a place of pilgrimage. The liturgy speaks of it as a 'pilgrimage of prayer and discipline' that 'we may grow in grace and learn to be your people once again'. In some ways Lent is less like following Jesus into the wilderness and more like following him down the mountain after the transfiguration and along the road, on which he immediately set out resolutely, his face towards Jerusalem and his eyes fixed on the cross. For the pilgrim is one who, travelling lightly and living simply, is on the move, with a destination on the horizon. For the Israelites it all went wrong when they lost sight of the destination and wandering set in. The Christian is not encouraged to wander during Lent, for it is not a static season, but has a dynamic and a direction. We are on a journey to share the paschal mystery. We try to make sense of it as we move towards it. But, even when we can't make sense of it, we know we are going to walk it with Jesus; and that can be life-changing. Our goal is not exactly Jerusalem, Canterbury or Lourdes, though the one we are looking for is to be found in all those places. Our goal is to be caught up in the love of God. If we keep that in view, we shall not wander. We shall be on pilgrimage to our holy city, walking gladly through the desert and grateful for the oases of prayer, sacrament and fruitful study that Lent provides along the way.

Yet the desert is also a place of repentance. 'For in these forty days you lead us into the desert of repentance that . . . we may grow in grace and learn to be your people once again.' It is important never to narrow down the meaning of 'repentance'. It is a bigger word than 'penitence', with which it is all too often identified. Penitence is itself an important word. Facing up to our sinfulness is necessary if we are to move on and the desert is often the place where it confronts us. There is too much in life to cushion us, there are too many people to be fooled by us, for us to have very often to face our sin, wilfulness, pretence and self-deception. It is when we go into the solitude of the desert and take away the props and the preoccupations that the unpalatable truth can become inescapable. So, yes, part of the Lenten wilderness is real penitence, such as might make you weep. But repentance is bigger than that. For it is a word – the Greek is *metanoia* – that means turning round and setting off in a new direction. Facing sin is all caught up in that, but is not the whole of it. What we discover in the desert is that sometimes, pilgrims as we are, we are on the wrong route, going in a false direction. That certainly happened to the Israelites of old. 'Turn back, turn round,' says the voice in our ear, 'make the desert a place of repentance'.

Almost paradoxically, the desert is at the same time the place of temptation. It was that for Jesus. There he was retreating into the solitude, with a sense of space, with the tranquillity of escaping from busyness into his desert place. And what happens? Not a sense of inward peace, not a confirmation of his vocation, such as he had had as he stood in the waters of the Jordan, not a wonderful refreshment, but a fight with the devil and a real crisis, though one through which he came. The desert of Lent can be like that for us too, sometimes at least. Strangely, it is when we most want to engage with God, with good, when we most want to grow in holiness, that evil can get hold of us, drive us into depression or despair, undermine our faith, tempt us to wickedness. The devil does prowl around, as scripture says, 'seeking whom he may devour' (1 Peter 5.8, AV), and the desert is the natural place for the devil, as well as for the angels. The wilderness experience is not all positive and the pursuit of holiness is a risky business.

Ultimately, however, the desert is a place of encounter and of grace. In the psalm that is entitled 'A Psalm of David, when he was in the Wilderness of Judah', the psalmist exclaims:

> O God, you are my God, I seek you,
> my soul thirsts for you;
> my flesh faints for you,
> as in a dry and weary land where there is no water.
> So I have looked upon you in the sanctuary,
> beholding your power and glory.
> Because your steadfast love is better than life,
> my lips will praise you.
> So I will bless you as long as I live;
> I will lift up my hands and call on your name.
> My soul is satisfied as with a rich feast,
> and my mouth praises you with joyful lips.
>
> Psalm 63.1–5

Yes, it is true that in the wilderness we find God's grace, for he loves us with an everlasting love. It is one of those divine surprises that the one whom we seek at the end of our pilgrimage, the one who is our goal and our glory, the one with whom we want to be reunited at Easter, cannot wait, because of his love for us. He cannot wait in the holy city to which we hope to come at our desert journey's end. Instead he comes to meet us. Indeed he inhabits the desert with us. In the wilderness we encounter him. In the simplicity, in the pilgrimage journey, in the repentance, we encounter him. In the oases, in the stoniest driest desert itself, even in the struggle with evil, we encounter him and are refreshed and renewed by him. In the wilderness we find his grace. He loves us there with an everlasting love. Even there in the desert with its Lenten fast, our soul is satisfied with a rich feast. In a strange way, stones are turned into bread by God himself.

As Isaiah puts it:

The wilderness and the dry land shall be glad,
the desert shall rejoice and blossom.

Isaiah 35.1

At the beginning of Lent, the invitation is a call to the desert. It may not immediately sound attractive, but it is a chance to escape for a while from the slavery of materialism, to fast and pray, to study and to be still, and to find in our wilderness a resting place that offers simplicity, pilgrimage, repentance, if needs be temptation, but ultimately encounter and grace.

TWO
Grain of Wheat

❧❧❧

The First Week of Lent

The psalmist speaks of eating ash like bread and mingling tears with drink (Psalm 102.9), and the beginning of Lent, with its wilderness, its reminder that we do not live by bread alone and its signing with ash as a sign of penitence and mortality, may seem to echo that. Yet, though the Church does give us ash, God, even in Lent, perhaps especially in Lent, continues to give us bread. If Lent is a pilgrimage, there needs to be food for the journey.

In the twelfth chapter of John's Gospel, Jesus says

The hour has come for the Son of Man to be glorified. Very truly, I tell you, unless a grain of wheat falls into the earth and dies, it remains just a single grain; but if it dies, it bears much fruit.

John 12.23–24

These words go to the heart of what Jesus is about and of what John wants us to understand. If we had to put together ten key truths of Christian faith, on my reckoning this would be among them: 'Unless a grain of wheat falls into the ground and dies, it remains just a single grain, but if it dies, it bears much fruit.'

Jesus is speaking of himself. He speaks these words when he has just spoken to the Father of the truth that the hour has now come for him to be glorified. It is John's great theme, that going to the cross is a sign of glory. John pursues it through the pages of his Gospel until Good Friday afternoon. Then Jesus will say in his dying breath 'It is finished' and the word he will use is not about the ordeal being over, but about a deed being accomplished; the nearest word in English is 'consummated'. For John it is glory all the way. That puzzled question that children ask – and maybe some adults too – 'But why is it Good Friday if it is the day they killed Jesus?' – elicits from the Jesus of John's Gospel a confident reply: 'Because I, if I am lifted up from the earth will draw everyone to myself' (see John 12.32). It is good because a grain of wheat, if it dies, yields a rich harvest.

What follows in the chapters of this Lenten pilgrimage explores his meaning in relation to the cross. But, first, I want to stay with the grain of wheat and to reflect upon it in relation to the Eucharist.

The New Testament in general and John's Gospel in particular is full of pointers to the Eucharist. Bread, wheat, harvest occur frequently, not always in stories we immediately associate with the Eucharist. But, especially in John's Gospel, we should always be on the look out for hints of the Eucharist. It is difficult to avoid noticing how, when the New Testament describes a shared meal, often there comes that same set of verbs that we associate with the Eucharist: he took, he gave thanks, he blessed, he gave. Whether it is Jesus feeding a multitude, or Jesus after his resurrection in the house at Emmaus or by the lakeside, or even Paul on board ship with a storm blowing and shipwreck imminent: taking, giving thanks, breaking, eating. These are the characteristic actions in which the Lord is recognized, known, experienced. John, who devotes a whole chapter of rich theology to the truth that Jesus is the Bread come down from heaven, the Bread of life, is always telling stories with eucharistic undertones. It is John who puts these words – 'unless a grain of wheat falls in the earth and dies' – in a response by Jesus to Andrew. And note that it is to Andrew, because back in chapter 6, John names Andrew as the one who brings to the Lord the lad with five barley loaves and two fish, but sighed 'What are they among so many?' Jesus took the bread and gave thanks and broke and gave to the disciples to feed the five thousand. I don't know for sure why, when the other Gospel writers name no names, John brings Andrew into the story by name, but I do know that, when reading John, the best policy is always to look for connections, to look below the surface, to look behind the story to uncover a deeper truth.

Look at the bread the little boy brings and see the bread the Son offers up to the Father. Look behind the sharing of bread and fish in a fellowship meal that was a kind of picnic and see that what the Lord offers in the body and the blood is the sharing, not of a picnic, but of redemption. Look behind the daily bread and see the bread of heaven. Always make connections. Always look below the surface. Always look behind the story.

Elizabeth Jennings, who was for me (until she died in 2001) the contemporary poet who wrote most tellingly from within the Christian tradition, published in 1996 a little book of poems entitled *In the Meantime*. There are a number of poems that reflect on the Eucharist, this one entitled simply 'Holy Communion':

> *There were some miracles intended to*
> *Save us from too much awe and wonderment.*
> *How simple are the things a priest must do*
> *To close Christ in a simple element.*
> *The Round of Bread is so*
>
> *Tiny, thin and white. It almost makes*
> *Us feel we must protect the Godhead when*
> *The Host looks like what any woman bakes*
> *For her small family. The wisest man*
> *Says nothing when he takes*
>
> *The little wafer. What can word*
> *Explain of this kind, gentle element?*
> *Silence is the way God is adored.*
> *Vaster than galaxies, this sacrament*
> *Holds Bethlehem's young Lord.*

'The wisest man says nothing when he takes the little wafer.' There were no wafers when John was writing his Gospel, only barley loaves and passover bread, but Elizabeth Jennings captures something of John's reticence about the Eucharist. The remarkable fact is that, although John's Gospel is full of eucharistic reference, he, alone among the Gospel writers, does not tell the story of the Last Supper. He tells of a gathering in an upper room, but describes only the washing of the feet, and does not mention the bread and the wine and the words of the Lord that the Church has repeated week in week out for two thousand years to remember him. There is in John a wise man who says nothing when he takes the bread. To say the words, even if they be the profoundest words on earth, is immediately to limit the meaning, in a sign without limit, where there are always more connections to be made and always new levels to find.

> What can word
> Explain of this kind, gentle element?
> Silence is the way God is adored.
> Vaster than galaxies, this sacrament
> Holds Bethlehem's young Lord.

says Elizabeth Jennings. And it puts me in mind of Teilhard de Chardin, the Jesuit theologian and scientist early in the last century, most of whose writings confuse my deeply unscientific mind, but whose 'Mass on the World', written eighty years ago, enables me to make connections. Teilhard de Chardin moves with ease in a world of elements and galaxies, and finding himself, a priest, in the Ordos Desert during a scientific expedition in 1923, with neither bread, nor wine, nor altar, prays:

> I will raise myself beyond these symbols, up to the pure majesty of the real itself; I, your priest, will make the

whole earth my altar and on it will offer you all the labours and sufferings of the world.

One by one I call before me the whole vast anonymous army of living humanity; those who surround me and support me though I do not know them; those who come, and those who go; above all, those who in office, laboratory and factory, through their vision of truth or despite their error, truly believe in the progress of earthly reality and who today will take up again their impassioned pursuit of the light.

This restless multitude, confused or orderly, the immensity of which terrifies us; this ocean of humanity whose slow, monotonous wave-flows trouble the hearts even of those whose faith is most firm: it is to this deep that I thus desire all the fibres of my being should respond. All the things in the world to which this day will bring increase; all those that will diminish; all those too that will die: all of them, Lord, I try to gather into my arms, so as to hold them out to you in offering. This is the material of my sacrifice; the only material you desire.

Receive, O Lord, this all-embracing host which your whole creation, moved by your magnetism, offers you at the dawn of a new day. This bread, our toil, is of itself, I know, but an immense fragmentation; this wine, our pain, is no more, I know, than a draught that dissolves. Yet in the very depths of this formless mass you have implanted – and this I am sure of, for I sense it – a desire, irresistible, hallowing, which makes us cry out, believer and unbeliever alike, 'Lord, make us one.'

Teilhard de Chardin, 'The Mass on the World',
Hymn of the Universe

Here is another profound making of connections. Teilhard de Chardin, in language reminiscent of Paul and his words in Romans that speak of the whole creation in travail, moves from bread and wine, or in his case the lack of it, to see the whole creation being offered up to the Father at the beginning of the new day. But what he sees is a fragmented world, a world of pain; that is what he sees offered up to the Father. He sees, in effect, not just broken bread, and not just the broken body of the Church, but the broken body of the world.

His words encourage us in this process of going behind and making connections. A fellowship picnic party connects with the Last Supper. The Last Supper connects with the pain and fragmentation – the broken body – of the cross. And the cross interacts with the travail of the creation. And if a grain of wheat falls into the ground and dies, it bears much fruit. And the fruit is not just my personal redemption or the redemption of the Church, but the salvation of the world – the 'restless multitude' and the 'ocean of humanity' of which Teilhard speaks. It's a wonderfully broad, embracing picture of redemption, but no broader than the one we affirm at every Eucharist when three times we say 'Lamb of God, you take away the sins of the world'.

We need to reflect sometimes along these lines – from the grain of wheat, which is so small you would hardly see it, to the cosmos so great you cannot begin to comprehend it – lest by its very familiarity we miss the wonder of the Eucharist. There is a danger that we domesticate it into something that does little more than bring us comfort or strength or imprison it in a kind of churchiness that imagines its concerns are only with the common life of Christians and the building up of the body of the Church. The Eucharist is about me and my personal spirituality, and indeed my salvation, and it is about the building up of the body of Christ, but it is also, and more fundamentally, about the cross that bears fruit for the whole world.

When I stand as a priest at the altar, nothing less than that ought to be on my heart. Each day we offer up to God all that he has made. Our God, the generous God prodigal with his love, cannot be satisfied with loving you and me, or even loving the Church (though he does that with total faithfulness). God so loves the world, his whole creation – loves and yearns and suffers and rejoices. And in the Eucharist we are caught up in that loving and yearning and suffering and rejoicing. The cross hovers over the cosmos. The grain of wheat is a tiny sign of a mighty harvest.

Jesus issues a number of invitations in the gospel story. There is the familiar 'Follow me' (Mark 1.17), first issued to the men who became his earliest disciples, and which subsequent generations have heard as an invitation to later followers too. 'Take up your cross' (Mark 10.21) is a harder, more immediately and obviously challenging call. As Christians we are marked with the cross, and we do try to take it, and hope and pray that, if one day we are asked to carry a heavier cross, we shall be given the grace to carry that too. And there are people we know whom we honour because they have walked patiently with heavy crosses to bear, sometimes through years and decades.

There is another invitation that I believe is as compelling as any other. It is related to that much repeated command at the supper on Maundy Thursday night to 'do this in remembrance of me'. The invitation is: 'Come and eat'.

In precisely that wording it is found only in one story, the Easter story where Jesus stands on the lakeside and calls to the fishermen-disciples to come and have breakfast.

> *When they had gone ashore, they saw a charcoal fire there, with fish on it, and bread. Jesus said to them, 'Bring some of the fish that you have just caught.' So Simon Peter went aboard and hauled the net ashore, full of large fish, a hundred and fifty-three of them; and though there were so many, the net was not torn. Jesus said to them, 'Come and have breakfast.' Now none of the disciples dared to ask him, 'Who are you?' because they knew it was the Lord. Jesus came and took the bread and gave it to them, and did the same with the fish.*
>
> John 21.9–13

Yet in another sense, Jesus is always saying 'Come and eat', whether it be to the crowd of 5000 in the desert, or to tax-collectors and sinners, or to the Twelve on the night before he died, or to the two friends after the walk to Emmaus. It is always 'Come and eat' and it is always bread that is on the menu.

In my own Christian pilgrimage, I have heard that invitation of Jesus more clearly than any other. Even when I have not been quite able to make out what following him might mean, even when I am somewhat resistant to taking up the cross or simply unable to fathom what is being asked of me, I have understood 'Come and eat' and have responded. I have knelt, I guess, at a thousand different altars and at least half-heard the unchanging words – 'This is my body, this is my blood, do this in remembrance of me' – and stretched out hands and taken what was offered and eaten it. Even when I have not been feeling very religious or prayerful, even when it has been difficult to concentrate on the words of the service because something else has been filling my mind, I keep hearing that invitation 'Come and eat'.

It is not always like that. Sometimes the worship is thrilling, the sense of God overwhelming, the experience of communion with him profound and real. Sometimes all distractions are banished. Christ is centre stage and I believe and trust, yearn and rejoice. But I do not believe that times like that are the only moments of grace. Mysteriously God can and does act when we are half-hearted, half-believing, half-uninterested, half-concentrating, providing we can produce just enough faith, staying power or openness to him to respond to that least complicated of invitations: 'Come and eat'.

But coming to eat is never an invitation to a comfortable supper party. Because of the fragmentation of the cross, there is cutting edge to this invitation.

Evelyn Underhill, that profoundly mystical writer of the last century, captures something of this in her poem, 'Corpus Christi'.

> Come, dear Heart!
> The fields are white to harvest: come and see
> As in a glass the timeless mystery
> Of love, whereby we feed
> On God, our bread indeed.
> Torn by the sickles, see him share the smart
> Of travailing Creation: maimed, despised,
> Yet by his lovers the more deeply prized
> Because for us he lays his beauty down –
> Last toll paid by Perfection for our loss!
> Trace on these fields his everlasting Cross,
> And o'er the stricken sheaves the Immortal Victim's
>   crown.
>
> From far horizons came a Voice that said,
> 'Lo! from the hand of Death take thou thy daily
>   bread.'
> Then I, awakening, saw
> A splendour burning in the heart of things:
> The flame of living love which lights the law
> Of mystic death that works the mystic birth.
> I knew the patient passion of the earth,
> Maternal, everlasting, whence there springs
> The Bread of Angels and the life of man.
> Now in each blade
> I, blind no longer, see
> The glory of God's growth: know it to be
> An earnest of the Immemorial Plan.

Yes, I have understood
How all these things are one great oblation made:
He on our altars, we on the world's rood.
Even as this corn,
Earth-born,
We are snatched from the sod,
Reaped, ground to grist,
Crushed and tormented in the Mills of God,
and offered at Life's hands, a living eucharist.

In Peter Coughlan and others (eds),

A Christian's Prayer Book

THREE
Water of Life

❧❧❧

The Second Week of Lent

The Bible begins with God and with water. Before ever there was land, garden, beast or human, there was water.

> *The earth was a formless void and darkness covered the face of the deep, while a wind from God swept over the face of the waters... And God said, 'Let there be a dome in the midst of the waters, and let it separate the waters from the waters.' So God made the dome and separated the waters that were under the dome from the waters that were above the dome. And it was so. God called the dome Sky... And God said, 'Let the waters under the sky be gathered together in one place, and let the dry land appear.'*

Genesis 1.2, 6–9

In the second account of creation, in the following chapter, with a different set of concerns, there is water again, this time a river flowing out of Eden to water the garden the Lord planted, a single river with four branches – the Pishon, the Gihon, the Tigris and the Euphrates (Genesis 2.10–14). Water from a single divine source is the means by which the Creator sustains life.

Scripture also ends with water. The garden may have given way to the city when we come to the last chapter of Revelation, but a tree is still important and so is a single source of water.

> *Then the angel showed me the river of the water of life, bright as crystal, flowing from the throne of God and of the Lamb through the middle of the street of the city. On either side of the river is the tree of life with its twelve kinds of fruit.*

Revelation 22.1–2

Water is significant also for Jesus and especially for that range of stories that we take on board through Lent. Our first Lent story may indeed be that of the time of trial in the wilderness, but we need to remember that it was the water experience that drove him there. The young man comes to the Jordan to be baptized by John and, though the Gospels tell it with subtle differences of emphasis, crucially he submits to baptism, goes down into the water and there hears the voice that acclaims him as the Beloved Son. The effect is to drive him into the wilderness (Mark 1.9–12). Mark uses a strong verb – there is a compulsion about the way the Spirit, who has descended upon him in the water, takes him off immediately into the desert. This water experience was indeed a powerful one.

Water is also part of the story at the other end of Lent. Our pilgrimage will bring us eventually to Calvary and to the cross. There, as John tells it, Jesus calls out from the cross 'I am thirsty' (John 19.28) and then, a few minutes later, when he has bowed his head and given up his spirit, *one of the soldiers pierced his side with a spear, and at once blood and water came out.*

John 19.34

It is an odd thing to mention unless it has theological significance. Why are we brought back to water at a moment like that? Elizabeth Jennings, in a poem called 'Christ on the Cross', explores the mind of the Lord as he hangs there:

Forgive them, Father, forgive them Father who
Is in my heart. How frightened she who stands,
My mother with my friend. The soldiers too,
Help me forgive them who have nailed my hands.
It seems so long ago

I taught in Temples. O the streams where John,
Another, poured the fountain on my head.
Father, I tell my mother that a son,
My friend, shall care for her when I am dead.
I am so dizzy on

This wood. The waters flow but now from me.
I have been chosen. Father, I am you
Who breathed, then sapped the great man-offered tree.
Spirit within me, there are risings too.
Father, forgive now, me.

Elizabeth Jennings, *Growing Points*

It may seem straightforward to associate Lent with thirst. It comes with the sense of the parched dryness of the desert. But to associate Lent with the gift of water may seem less obvious. Yet it is a recurring theme in the season of Lent and the reason is not hard to discover. The origins of Lent lie in the period when those who were to be baptized at Easter went into the final phase of their preparation. Water stories like that of the Samaritan woman at the well at Sychar (John 4.1–42) and that of the blind man by the Pool of Siloam (John 9.1–41) find their place as gospel readings on Sundays in Lent because of their part in the preparation of candidates for baptism. In the case of the Samaritan woman, Jesus speaks of himself as 'living water' that will become 'a spring of water gushing up to eternal life' (John 4.10, 14). In the case of the Pool of Siloam, it was when water was brought to the temple from the pool as part of the ritual of the Feast of Tabernacles that Jesus cried out 'Let anyone who is thirsty come to me, and let the one who believes in me drink' (John 7.37).

The candidates for baptism were being prepared for their entry into the life-giving water. It is easy for us to lose sight of the powerful imagery of the water, for Christian history and liturgical practice have made little of the water of baptism. Where, in the early centuries, new Christians were taken to the river or, a little later, to a separate 'room' of the church, the baptistery, where they would go down steps into sufficient water that a person might drown, we have very often celebrated baptism with insufficient water to drown a flea, let alone a man or woman. The medieval fonts in many of our older churches allow for quite a generous quantity of water; they date from an era when all baptisms were of infants and the babies were dunked in the water of the font, so that the water could indeed envelop them. But often such fonts nowadays are never filled to the brim and later fonts are often more like bird baths. Rarely are candidates dipped in the water; water is smeared on their head rather meanly and, as often as not, immediately wiped off again. People asked about the symbolism of baptism are as likely to focus on naming, making the sign of the cross or receiving a candle as on the plunging in the water that signals what the sacrament is all about.

So what is it all about? It is an extraordinarily rich symbol, many-layered in its meaning. The prayer that the priest prays over the water at baptism, and which reaches its climax in an invocation of the Holy Spirit, exists in a number of versions, but nearly all of them point to this rich tapestry of meaning.

We thank you, almighty God, for the gift of water
to sustain, refresh and cleanse all life.
Over the water the Holy Spirit moved in the
    beginning of creation.
Through water you led the children of Israel
from slavery in Egypt to freedom in the Promised
    Land.
In water your Son Jesus Christ received the baptism
    of John
and was anointed by the Holy Spirit as the Messiah,
    the Christ,
to lead us from the death of sin to newness of life.

We thank you, Father, for the water of baptism.
In it we are buried with Christ in his death.
By it we share in his resurrection.
Through it we are reborn by the Holy Spirit.
Therefore, in joyful obedience to your Son,
we baptize into his fellowship those who come to
  him in faith.

Now sanctify this water that, by the power of your
  Holy Spirit,
they may be cleansed from sin and born again.
Renewed in your image, may they walk by the light
  of faith
and continue for ever in the risen life of Jesus
  Christ . . .

Prayer over the Water, *Common Worship*

The references to Jesus are in relation to his baptism, his anointing with the Spirit, his death and his resurrection. For the Christian the meaning lies in relation to birth, to cleansing, to refreshment and life, and to death and resurrection. From womb to tomb and beyond, the water of baptism has something to say.

In the 'breaking of the waters' we emerge from the womb into physical life. The water of the font becomes the spiritual equivalent, for it is the place of rebirth. Even a teacher of Israel found that difficult to comprehend, but Jesus himself became the teacher of Nicodemus, who came to him by night, and helped him to make some sense of being 'born again'. Jesus said to Nicodemus,

'Very truly, I tell you, no one can see the kingdom of God without being born anew.' Nicodemus said to him, 'How can anyone be born after having grown old? Can one enter a second time into the mother's womb and be born?' Jesus answered, 'Very truly, I tell you, no one can enter the kingdom of God without being born of water and Spirit. What is born of the flesh is flesh, and what is born of the Spirit is spirit. Do not be astonished that I said to you, "You must be born anew."'

John 3.3–7

The water of baptism is about our rebirth. It is also about our cleansing. It is the one aspect of the water that people have held on to at the expense of the others, though even then it has led people into some theological confusion as they wrestle with the idea of original sin and the innocence of new-born infants. The sense of wiping the slate clean, of leaving behind the old life and embarking on the new, cleansed and healed, is much easier to appreciate in relation to an adult candidate and, in our post-Christendom society, adult candidates for baptism are more common. The Second Book of Kings tells the story of Naaman, the Syrian commander, who is cleansed of his leprosy by immersing himself seven times in the Jordan (2 Kings 5.1–15a), but it is spiritual cleansing that is signified by the water of baptism. With the psalmist we find ourselves saying

Have mercy on me, O God,
   according to your steadfast love;
according to your abundant mercy
   blot out my transgressions.

Wash me thoroughly from my iniquity,
and cleanse me from my sin.

Psalm 51.1–2

Yet, important as that is, and it seems more so in the Lenten desert of repentance, it is not the primary emphasis of Christian baptism as we receive it from the New Testament. It is the emphasis in John's baptism on the Jordan, which was indeed 'a baptism of repentance, for the remission of sins'. But baptism into Christ is something different.

The Christian emphasis is much more on refreshment, life and growth. We wash in water, but we also need to drink water if we are to survive, to live and to grow. Certainly that comes through in the conversation with the woman by Jacob's well at Sychar. It comes through even more strongly when Jesus stands up on the last great day of the Feast of Tabernacles and cries out in the temple

Let anyone who is thirsty come to me, and let the one who believes in me drink. As the scripture has said, 'Out of his belly shall flow rivers of living water.' Now he said this about the Spirit, which believers in him were to receive.

John 7.37–39

It is a powerful passage. The fact that Jesus stands and cries out gives his words particular authority. It is a wonderful invitation to find life in him. The alleged quotation from the Old Testament that no one can identify is a puzzle and the 'his' of 'out of his belly' may be the believer or may be the holy city of Jerusalem.

Either way, the source of the water is Jesus, and it is not a drop in the ocean, but flowing rivers of living water. It is an extravagant image signifying vibrant health and life. The water of baptism is entry into the good and abundant life, with constant streams of refreshment. It links, of course, with the vision in Revelation 22 of the 'river of the water of life' with which the Bible ends.

But even this very positive image is not the heart of the matter. For the water also spells death – drowning – and new life. It's quite a subtle idea or, more exactly, it comes to us by a complex route. For the Israelite people the overwhelming experiences of divine activity, of redemption, were in the water. It happened more than once. First there was Noah, who when all the other inhabitants of the world perished, was saved with his family as they kept safe on board the ark of gopher wood. The Old Testament tells the story in Genesis 6–9, but the First Letter of Peter identifies the story with Christian baptism. Jesus Christ

> went and made a proclamation to the spirits in prison, who in former times did not obey, when God waited patiently in the days of Noah, during the building of the ark, in which a few, that is, eight persons, were saved through water. And baptism, which this prefigured, now saves you – not as the removal of dirt from the body, but as an appeal to God for a good conscience through the resurrection of Jesus Christ.
>
> 1 Peter 3.19–21

Then there was the Exodus from Egypt led by Moses, the journey that brought them through the Red Sea, in which they would have been drowned (as the pursuing Egyptians were) were it not for divine intervention, and a later journey across the Jordan into the promised land. The experience here was of leaving behind the old life, passing through the waters that ought to have been death-dealing, but which turned out to be life-giving, and into a new future full of promise. The water became the symbol of a kind of death and resurrection.

So, for all that Jesus died on the dry wood of the cross, the tradition speaks of him going 'through the deep waters of death'. For the Christian the death and resurrection, because they bring salvation, become the new Exodus experience. The New Testament then has only one further step to go. Passing through the waters of baptism, the Christian identifies with Noah and his family and Moses and his people, but even more with Jesus in his death and resurrection. Paul urges this understanding on the Christians at Rome when he asks:

> *Do you not know that all of us who have been baptized into Christ Jesus were baptized into his death? Therefore we have been buried with him by baptism into death, so that, just as Christ was raised from the dead by the glory of the Father, so we too might walk in newness of life.*

Romans 6.3–4

One of the invitations of the Christian through Lent

is therefore to meditate on water, spring, fountain, river and flood and to explore their meaning in relation to the Christian discipleship to which our baptism has committed us. We need to engage with the many-layered mystery of the water through which God brings about rebirth and cleansing, gives life and growth and rescues from death. We need to see how, just as the Spirit is portrayed as the wind, whether in creation or at Pentecost, it is also identified with the water. That meditation will bring us to Holy Week, to another water story full of baptismal associations. Jesus gets down on his knees and washes the feet of his apostles, so that they may be clean and be part of his fellowship. It will bring us to Easter, when, if we are fortunate, we will witness the baptism of new Christians, and almost certainly have the opportunity ourselves to renew our baptismal vows. It will be absolutely the right time to do so, because through Lent we shall have been preparing to go with him through the death and resurrection experience that our baptism celebrates. We shall be all the more ready to try to live that strange pattern of 'living through dying' to which our baptism has committed us and which the world finds it so hard to understand.

In the middle of the twentieth century, Eric Milner-White, who was Dean of York, wrote this meditation, which he called 'Fountain of Life':

> O my God, from thee I proceed;
> to thee I belong;
> thee adore.

Thou art the fountain of my whole being,
fountain of a thousand springs
of mercy, pardon and loving kindness;
source of light, well of grace;
thee I adore.

Thine is the voice of many waters
now loud, now low, and lovely always,
calling me to thy work and mine,
calling to faith, to hope, to resolve,
calling to love, the greatest of these;
thee I adore.

Fountain of joy and melody in the heart,
fountain of peace and quietness of soul,
fountain of will to do thy will,
thee I adore.

Spring and fountain and river and flood,
O God most holy,
from thee I proceed,
to thee I belong,
my beginning, my Goal, my all,
thee I adore.

Eric Milner-White, *My God, My Glory*

FOUR
Fruit of the Vine

❧◗◖❧

The Third Week of Lent

We need to picture Jesus in the upper room on the night before he died, keeping passover with friends (at least that is how three of the evangelists see it). He has taken a loaf of bread, blessed it, broken it and given it to them. And now he takes a cup of wine. Again he gives thanks, gives it to them and they all drink from it. 'This is my blood of the covenant, which is poured out for many,' he says (Mark 14.24). Few sentences are more familiar to the Christian, hearing them repeated at every Eucharist. 'Cup', 'wine', 'blood' – we are used to the association of these words. We may even think we know the punch-line that will follow, 'Do this in remembrance of me'. Jesus does go on, but that is not what he says (though those words do belong within the accounts of the supper). What he does say is less familiar.

> Truly, I tell you, I will never again drink of the fruit of the vine until that day when I drink it new in the kingdom of God.

Mark 14.25

'The fruit of the vine' – it is a striking phrase, Jewish in style, but not found elsewhere in scripture. It is also a puzzling sentence, whether in the form Mark gives it to us, or in Luke's variant ('until the kingdom of God comes', Luke 22.18) or Matthew's ('until that day when I drink it new with you in my Father's kingdom', Matthew 26.29). In terms of word associations, it brings into play, alongside 'cup', 'wine' and 'blood', the words 'vine' and 'kingdom' and, if we let these five words interact, we find rich associations that lead us deeper into the mystery of Christ's death and resurrection.

But what does it mean, that the Lord will not drink of the fruit of the vine until he drinks it new in the kingdom of God? Eduard Schweizer, in his commentary on Mark's Gospel, has this to say:

> *The Lord's Supper would not be the Lord's Supper without the anticipation of the final end. To be 'present' at this table fellowship is to be 'present' in the future. Fellowship in the present time is genuine fellowship simply because it occurs in the presence of Christ. For this reason it is impossible to conceive of such fellowship apart from its accomplishment in Christ's future, when being 'with Christ' will have become a reality. This is the basis of the joyous character of the Lord's Supper . . . Such joy is possible only when the settled conviction persists that what happens now in a symbolic manner in the midst of temptation will be fulfilled as a gift in the future Kingdom of God. With this kind of anticipation the church celebrated the Supper as the table fellowship which God had given them in the present time but which was looking forward to greater fulfilment in the future.*
>
> *The Good News According to Mark*

We are looking in on the night before Jesus died and the agony of Gethsemane is only minutes away. We have talk of blood to be shed and know that will be fulfilled the very next day. Yet it seems that we should talk about festivity and that we should look ahead, not just a few hours to the cross, but into a far-off future when the kingdom of God comes.

Christian experience suggests that we should indeed do that, for every Eucharist holds together three moods and attitudes: festivity, anticipation and remembrance. They might at first seem to be in conflict, but remarkably the Eucharist holds them together in subtle ways.

The Eucharist is festivity, because it celebrates both the resurrection and also the banquet of the Lamb (of which more in a moment). But it is festivity for another reason. It is festivity because, at a much more basic human level, it is a party. If bread stands naturally for human toil and labour, the work of our hands, wine more easily stands for human joy and fellowship. The psalmist gets it right when he says to God

> You . . . bring forth food from the earth,
>   and wine to gladden the human heart,
> oil to make the face shine,
>   and bread to strengthen the human heart.
>
> Psalm 104.14–15

Bread is for strength, but wine is for gladness. Whatever else the Eucharist is, it is the gathering of friends around a table with a bottle of decent wine. It

has echoes of the first miracle at Cana, where Jesus
wants there to be enough wine and more at the wed-
ding feast, for his father is a God of joy and gladness
(John 2.1–11). The very word 'celebration', that we
use of the Eucharist, is a good hint that there needs
to be something of the party about our sharing in
the basic human activity – sharing in food, drink and
fellowship. The early Church certainly saw it like this.
'They broke bread from house to house,' says Luke in
the Acts, 'and ate their food with glad and generous
hearts, praising God' (Acts 2.46–47).

The Eucharist is also a daring anticipation of the
kingdom. Talk of the kingdom of God is sometimes,
of course, about establishing a kingdom on earth,
sometimes about a kingdom in heaven, sometimes
about making the one mirror the other. The Bible
imagines the consummation of all things in a feast.
Isaiah expects a banquet with fine wines:

> On this mountain the LORD of hosts will make for
>   all peoples
>   a feast of rich food, a feast of well-aged wines,
>   of rich foods filled with marrow, of well-aged wines
>   strained clear.
> And he will destroy on this mountain
>   the shroud that is cast over all peoples,
>   the sheet that is spread over all nations;
>   he will swallow up death for ever.
>
> Isaiah 25.6–7

The Book of Revelation looks to the same banquet
at the end of time, but now with Christ centre stage,

when the angel says 'Blessed are those who are invited to the marriage supper of the Lamb' (Revelation 19.9). When Jesus speaks, in Matthew's version, of drinking the fruit of the vine 'new with you in my Father's kingdom' (26.29), he seems to be looking to this kind of heavenly feast, one which he will share with those who have been his followers. Perhaps in Luke he means something more to do with a kingdom to come on earth. But the Eucharist is about joining earth and heaven. The way in to the angelic song, 'Holy, holy, holy . . .', invites us never to let our worship be earthbound, but to allow ourselves to be transported to the heavenly table, holding present and future together in a way that transcends time.

Yet there is no escaping the fact that the Eucharist, though it looks forward and joins present and future, also looks back and joins past and present. That is the meaning of the immensely strong word, *anamnesis*, that we translate as 'remembrance'. On that Thursday night, Jesus put a new slant on a festive meal that anticipated heaven by saying of the wine in the cup, 'This is my blood, poured out for many.' There is no avoiding that, in so doing, he makes of the cup of wine a strangely contradictory sign. It is the cup of gladness, but it is also the cup of sacrifice. Through the eyes of faith it becomes his blood that he will shed on the cross. He is the one who turned water into wine, but on Good Friday John will tell us that from his side flowed blood and water (John 19.34).

There is a direct simplicity about Josiah Conder's

nineteenth-century hymn, in which he addresses
Christ as the Vine:

> *Vine of heaven, thy blood supplies*
> *This blest cup of sacrifice;*
> *'Tis thy wounds our healing give;*
> *To thy cross we look and live:*
> *Thou our life! O let us be*
> *Rooted, grafted, built on thee.*
>
> 'Bread of heaven, on thee we feed', *New English Hymnal*

Festivity, anticipation and remembrance all play their
part in the Eucharist. But, as Josiah Conder reminds
us, Jesus not only takes the cup, speaks of the wine as
his blood, and looks forward to drinking the fruit of
the vine in the kingdom, but also calls himself 'the
vine'. 'I am the true vine,' he says, 'and my Father is
the vinegrower' (John 15.1). In so doing, he claims
for himself, as so often, a title that has belonged
before to Israel itself.

> *You brought a vine out of Egypt;*
> *   you drove out the nations and planted it.*
> *You cleared the ground for it;*
> *   it took deep root and filled the land . . .*
> *Turn again, O Lord of hosts;*
> *   look down from heaven and see;*
> *have regard for this vine,*
> *   the stock that your right hand planted.*
>
> Psalm 80.8–9, 14–15

Just as the people of God were the 'suffering servant'
and Jesus makes that his own and carries all its

implications in his own body, so now he claims to be the vine that God has planted; it is, of course, a vine that will be cut down.

These words resonate with the parable Jesus himself tells of a vineyard owner, which itself echoes words from Isaiah's song of an unfruitful vineyard:

> My beloved had a vineyard
>   on a very fertile hill.
> He dug it and cleared it of stones,
>   and planted it with choice vines;
> he built a watchtower in the midst of it,
>   and hewed out a wine vat in it;
> he expected it to yield grapes,
>   but it yielded wild grapes . . .
> And now I will tell you
>   what I will do to my vineyard.
> I will remove its hedge,
>   and it shall be devoured;
> I shall break down its wall,
>   and it shall be trampled down.
>
> Isaiah 5.1–2, 5–6

The vineyard is faithless Israel. The parable that Jesus himself tells draws heavily on this Old Testament picture. Standing in the temple, after turning out the merchants and the money-changers, he tells a story of a landowner 'who planted a vineyard, put a fence around it, dug a wine press in it, and built a watchtower'. The parallel with Isaiah is precise. Jesus wants everybody to know that the vineyard is Israel. And then his parable develops its own story. The landowner leased the vineyard to tenants

> and went to another country. When the harvest time had come, he sent his slaves to the tenants to collect his produce. But the tenants seized his slaves and beat one, killed another, and stoned another. Again he sent other slaves, more than the first; and they treated them in the same way. Finally he sent his son to them, saying, 'They will respect my son.' But when the tenants saw the son, they said to themselves, 'This is the heir; come, let us kill him and get his inheritance.' So they seized him, threw him out of the vineyard, and killed him.
>
> Matthew 21.33–39

Jesus, who is himself the vine, who will drink the fruit of the vine in the kingdom, is the one who will tread the winepress alone, as Isaiah puts it (Isaiah 63.3), and will be taken outside and killed, though he is the vineyard owner's son. The ideas overlap and are not entirely consistent. But they are related and each of them helps us to understand why Jesus takes the cup of wine into his hands at the supper and says what he does.

It is helpful also to pursue a little further the relationship between the vine and the kingdom. For Jesus develops the vine analogy, so that it speaks not only of himself and of his Father, but also of his disciples. He is the vine and they are the branches. The context of his teaching about the vine is important. It is the way in to what he has to say about love, including love for one's friends. There is little doubt that the fruit he is looking for, without which the branches are thrown away and wither, is love.

> *I do not call you servants any longer, because the servant does not know what the master is doing; but I have called you friends, because I have made known to you everything that I have heard from my Father. You did not choose me but I chose you. And I appointed you to go and bear fruit, fruit that will last, so that the Father will give you whatever you ask him in my name. I am giving you these commands so that you may love one another.*

John 15.15–17

And perhaps this is a clue as to how we may relate the fruit of the vine to the coming of the kingdom, as Jesus did at the supper. For, if the kingdom is to be established on the earth, its coming will be a slow process of patient love. Its values will be quite the opposite of those who beat and stoned the slaves and took the son outside the vineyard to kill him. It will be set forward by those who are grafted into Christ and go on bearing the fruit of fragile love until the kingdom in heaven breaks through on earth. It is the vine-grower's kingdom.

I sense something of that in a Brazilian prayer by Rubem Alves:

> *My God, I need to have signs of your grace.*
> *Serve me your sacraments,*
> *the first fruits of your kingdom.*

I thirst for smiles,
for sweet odours,
for soft words,
for firm gestures,
for truth and goodness,
and for triumphs
(no matter how small)
of justice.

You know, O God, how hard it is to survive captivity
without any hope of the Holy City.
Sing to us, God, the songs of the promised land.
Serve us your manna in the desert.

Let there be in some place,
a community of men, women, elderly, children, and
    new-born babies
as a first fruit,
as our appetiser,
and our embrace of the future.

In Janet Morley (ed.), *Bread of Tomorrow*

The sacraments as the first fruits of the kingdom –
that's a fine picture. But it is not just a picture for
heaven, but a yearning for the signs of the kingdom
on earth. The community that may itself also be the
first fruits, the embrace of the future, is likely to be
the community of the vine and the branches, where
the fruit is love. This is why the recovery in recent
generations of the corporate nature of the Eucharist
has been so important. Those who gather around
the table of the Lord and daringly anticipate the feast

of heaven constitute the community of vine and branches that bears fruit in growing the kingdom of God around them.

In all this there is a challenge to the Christian to see so much more on the altar than a cup of wine. There is this rich harvest of ideas to reap, almost like a cluster of grapes in itself. But, beyond that, there is the challenge in the fact that we are invited, not just to meditate on the cup, fruitful as that is, but to drink from it. Jesus asked James and John whether they were able to drink the cup that he would drink and to be baptized with the baptism with which he was baptized. They answered that they were able (Mark 10.39). To those who share his baptism, he still asks, 'Are you able to drink the cup that I drink?' That cup has all those Last Supper associations with the wine, the blood, the vine and the kingdom, but also with the struggle in Gethsemane straight after the meal, in which Jesus prayed 'Remove this cup from me; yet, not what I want, but what you want' (Mark 14.36). The cup is nothing less than an acceptance of the way of the cross. Eric Milner-White says of it:

> *this the cup of pardon, healing, gladness, strength,*
> *that, whoso drinketh, thirsteth not again.*
>
> 'The Lord's Supper', *My God, My Glory*

Brim full with the fruit of the vine, it is a cup of con-tradictions – a common cup, a shared cup, the pledge of inclusiveness and a sign of festivity, of sacrifice and of the coming kingdom.

In one of the finest eucharistic hymns of the twentieth century, Richard Parsons wrote:

O stream of love unending,
Poured from the one true vine,
With our weak nature blending
The strength of life divine;
Our thankful faith confessing
In thy life-blood outpoured,
We drink this cup of blessing
And praise thy name, O Lord.

'We hail thy presence glorious', *New English Hymnal*

FIVE
Mountain of His Holiness

❧❧❧

The Fourth Week of Lent

Great is the LORD, and greatly to be praised
in the city of our God,
in the mountain of his holiness.

Psalm 48.1 AV

It is only the King James version of scripture that
speaks of 'the mountain of his holiness'. The Book of
Common Prayer speaks of 'his holy hill' and most of
the newer translations of 'his holy mountain'. But it
is a striking phrase – 'the mountain of his holiness' – and refers, of course, to Mount Zion. In the life
of Jesus there are a number of mountains or hills that
might claim that title. Three at least belong to the
final stage of his ministry – the mountain of transfiguration, the mount of Olives and the hill of
Golgotha. It is the first of these that helps us, at this
stage in the Lenten pilgrimage, to draw nearer to the
events we are preparing to celebrate.

Matthew tells the story like this:

Six days later, Jesus took with him Peter and James and
his brother John and led them up a high mountain by
themselves. And he was transfigured before them, and
his face shone like the sun, and his clothes became
dazzling white. Suddenly there appeared to them Moses

*and Elijah, talking with him. Then Peter said to Jesus,
'Lord, it is good for us to be here; if you wish, I will
make three dwellings here, one for you, one for Moses,
and one for Elijah.' While he was still speaking, suddenly a bright cloud overshadowed them, and from
the cloud a voice said, 'This is my Son, the Beloved;
with him I am well pleased; listen to him!' When the
disciples heard this, they fell to the ground and were
overcome by fear.*

Matthew 17.1–6

It is a scene of power and beauty. But how does it
help on the journey to the cross? The answer lies in
its precise place in the development of the ministry
of Jesus. It is indeed pivotal, for the transfiguration
and its sequel are enveloped in predictions of the
passion. The gospel writers tell it in this sequence.
First Peter declares Jesus to be the Christ. In response
Jesus gives the first prediction of his passion. Then
comes the transfiguration. Jesus responds to that
revelation with a second prediction of the passion.
Coming down from the mountain he is involved in
a particularly difficult healing. His response is a third
prediction of what awaits him in Jerusalem.

For the best part of three years, since his baptism
in the River Jordan and his experience in the wilderness where he has thought through his vocation and
wrestled with evil, Jesus has been an itinerant
preacher and healer, going hither and thither, pro-
claiming the kingdom of God.

But now something tells him that there is to be a
sea change in that ministry. The itinerant phase is

over. Now there is to be one clear objective to be followed in faithfulness. And so, in a way that certainly flags up the change of mood, Jesus asks the very question that until now he has seemed to do everything to avoid. 'Who am I?' 'Who do you think I am?' They were at Caesarea Philippi when he posed the question. It was Peter who came out with it: 'You are the Christ, the Messiah, the Son of the living God' (Matthew 16.16). It was an amazing declaration, quite the most daring human affirmation that had been made about Jesus. A key moment – the truth is out, the truth has been spoken.

Yet Jesus only half accepts it. He calls Simon Peter 'blessed', for it is the Father who has revealed it. Yet he goes on to talk of himself, not as the Christ, but as the 'Son of Man', a strangely ambiguous title, and to speak of suffering:

> *From that time on, Jesus began to show his disciples that he must go to Jerusalem and undergo great suffering at the hands of the elders and chief priests and scribes, and be killed, and on the third day be raised. And Peter took him aside and began to rebuke him, saying, 'God forbid it, Lord! This must never happen to you.' But he turned and said to Peter, 'Get behind me, Satan! You are a stumbling block to me; for you are setting your mind not on divine things but on human things'.*

> Matthew 16.21–23

Peter, in a sense, has blown it. He has produced this wonderful affirmation and has demonstrated a perception beyond that of others. Yet he ends up being called Satan, with echoes of Jesus in the wilderness in conflict with the devil. The great human affirmation turns out to fall far short of the providence of God. And what it has elicited from Jesus – who presumably knew that the time was ripe – is the first of these predictions that he must suffer. The evangelist presents it in such a way that he portrays Jesus as gradually introducing this strange new idea to the disciples that they might make sense of it.

But then there is a change of scene. Jesus takes Peter and James and John up the mountain. It matters not which mountain it was; the New Testament is content simply to call it 'the holy mountain' and the traditional association of it with Tabor is probably mistaken. The story that follows is full of symbolic language rich in meaning. Not a single word is there by chance. Even the beginning, 'six days later', picks up on the six days when the cloud covered the glory of God on Mount Sinai when Moses went up to meet with the Lord. And here is Moses again, and Elijah with him, the representatives of the law and the prophets. Or so they would have been understood by the witnesses of the transfiguration. Moses the law-giver standing for the God who speaks through tradition, through order, through established ways. Elijah the prophet standing for the God of surprises, who speaks through the outsider, with freshness and unpredictability. And here they are, both of them, law and prophet, establishment and outsider, both affirming Jesus.

Then comes the voice of God: 'This is my Son, the Beloved; with him I am well pleased; listen to him!' You cannot help recalling – perhaps even Jesus could not help recalling – that the last time we heard words like these was right back at the beginning, when Jesus came to the Jordan. The words were the same: 'This is my Son, the Beloved; with him I am well pleased.' But at that earlier time the voice did not add 'Listen to him'. The baptism had marked the beginning of the itinerant ministry. At least it almost did so; there was only the delay of the encounter with the devil, and then it began. Could it be that the transfiguration was to mark the beginning of the new focused ministry, Jerusalem in his sights, to which Jesus now turned?

Yes, but not until this strange mysterious mountain-top experience had revealed to the disciples, and perhaps confirmed for Jesus himself, who it was who would now set out renewed. For the mountain-top vision told of the lordship of Christ, of his glory and of his holiness.

His lordship was revealed to the disciples at the transfiguration with very great clarity. It was not a new idea. Simon Peter at least had grasped it at Caesarea Philippi with his 'You are the Christ'. But, for all that, their understanding of Jesus seems to have been of a remarkable man, an outstanding human being. But on the holy mountain, when the cloud came down, the voice spoke and the words of the Father were heard, then they knew. This was the Son of God. This was the Lord. This was someone to whom they must relate in a way quite different from all their other relationships. They must place themselves under his lordship, his authority, his protection, and recognize themselves to be his. On the mountain they were given the grace to know him as he was and as he is. And that is the way that people today need to know him. He is not some past teacher, holy man, or sage. He is not some dead hero or exemplar of human living. He is, 'is' not 'was', God's anointed one, the Lord, and, if we can see that and experience it, like the disciples on the holy mountain, we know that we too can place ourselves under his lordship, his authority, his protection, and recognize ourselves to be his.

If the transfiguration revealed something about lordship, it also revealed something about glory. To be with Jesus, as Peter and James and John had been for nearly three years, was to be with one who was, in many ways, a failure. What had he achieved? There were some people who had been healed, rather more who had been moved, encouraged or impressed. But there was hostility and misunderstanding; nothing much changed. There were the twelve men and some women, but most of those who came to hear Jesus went away again. There was no mass movement. It certainly did not look as if the Roman occupying forces were to be challenged. How would things continue? Much the same? The itinerant ministry, a little teaching here, a little healing there, around the towns of Galilee?

But then comes the transfiguration, and it seems to say: 'Don't be fooled. This may not look much like a success story. But there is indeed glory here nonetheless.' The cloud coming down, the voice from heaven, the word of the Father, all come as a confirmation that Jesus is doing his will, is on the right path. They reveal the Lord as one who shares the glory of the Father. For God reveals his own glory on the mountain and shows at the same time that Jesus is part of it. That comes across to the disciples – they perceive how things really are. Appearances can be deceptive, but here is the truth. This is the only-begotten Son of the Father who shares his glory. But it also seems to come across to Jesus himself. It is as if he also perceives the glory, and finds the path to it. For he comes down from the mountain, pursuing his path of misunderstanding, failure and plain rejection with a new kind of vigour, as if now he can see that this really is the way to glory.

The mountain is also the 'mountain of his holiness'. There is about this story a great sense of awe, of mystery, of holiness. There is the cloud, the voice, the bright dazzling light, the inappropriate impulsive words of Peter overwhelmed by the experience. It was for the disciples a kind of heavenly vision. There were Moses and Elijah, and there was Jesus almost, as it were, at the right hand of the Father. A vision of heaven and an anticipation of the Lord risen and ascended. What a jolt to those who lived daily in his company and had perhaps come to take him for granted, this very human Jesus, hot and sweaty and tired like the rest of them. Suddenly he is caught up in the holiness of heaven itself.

And it was not only the three disciples. We are told by Mark that, when he came down the mountain, as soon as they saw Jesus the whole crowd were overcome with awe (Mark 9.14). Jesus still had heaven written all over his face as he came down the mountain. There was something awesome and holy about him. It was as if the disciples, in generous measure, and the crowd, to a smaller degree, had been given a glimpse of what was to be, a window into heaven.

Lordship, glory and holiness were all revealed in that passing moment of revelation. The disciples would have clung on to it if they could. Peter's plan to build three dwellings was a ploy to extend the experience. But Ann Lewin reminds us that moments of glory are rarely more than glimpses.

> *A moment of blinding perception –*
> *It would be good to stay there,*
> *But clutch it, and it's gone.*
> *They come unheralded,*
> *Those moments of dazzling clarity,*
> *And leave us as suddenly.*
>
> *As well try catch the kingfisher*
> *Darting through stillness.*
>
> *Be thankful for its jewelled beauty,*
> *And keep awake, alert.*
>
> 'Transfiguration', *Candles and Kingfishers*

'Keep awake' – there is an anticipation of the next mountain challenge.

The experience of glory upon the mountain of transfiguration, for all its wonder, is short-lived. Very soon Jesus is alone, telling the disciples to say nothing to anyone as they come back down the mountain. The disciples are wanting to clarify the experience, so they ask about Elijah. Jesus gives them an answer – Elijah has come; they understood that he meant John the Baptist – but takes the conversation off in a different direction:

> Elijah has already come, and they did not recognize him, but they did to him whatever they pleased. So also the Son of Man is about to suffer at their hands.
>
> Matthew 17.12

He's brought them back to that again, to his suffering. He needs to tell them. The voice in the cloud has added those key words that were first heard at the baptism: 'Listen to him.' Listen to him and what does he say? He says that the Son of Man is about to suffer. That is what they are to hear and to try to understand.

They come to the bottom of the mountain. Here they find a crowd and at the heart of it a man with his epileptic son, and the other disciples failing to cure him. This looks like another straightforward healing story and maybe it was like that for the father and his son. But it was certainly not for the evangelist and probably not for those who looked on with eyes of insight. Remember the baptism. There Jesus hears the voice from heaven, engages in conflict with the devil, and then begins his ministry. And look at what is happening now. Jesus hears the same voice from heaven and again engages in conflict with the devil. We see only a sadly troubled epileptic child. The evangelist saw another conflict with the devil: 'Jesus rebuked the demon' – it's another 'Get behind me, Satan'. And then, having once again mastered the evil one, the new phase of his ministry can begin.

It may be that in this encounter, there is not only the flash back to the wilderness, but also the anticipation of struggles to come. There is the struggle on the Mount of Olives, where, supper ended, Jesus comes into the Garden of Gethsemane with the same trio of disciples who have been on the holy mountain.

> He took with him Peter and the two sons of Zebedee, and began to be grieved and agitated. Then he said to them, 'I am deeply grieved, even to death; remain here, and stay awake with me.' And going a little farther, he threw himself on the ground and prayed, 'My Father, if it is possible, let this cup pass from me; yet not I want, but what you want.'
>
> Matthew 26.37–39

Is this the 'opportune time' when the devil would return, which Luke had predicted (Luke 4.13)? If so, once again, just as at the foot of the mountain with the epileptic boy, it is the power of prayer that wins through and puts the devil to flight. It is another mountain of resolute holiness.

Beyond that there is the struggle on another hilltop, that wild and lonely place where he will, yet once more, take on the devil and win. Golgotha and the

cross are the final engagement with the forces of evil.
That also, as John keeps urging upon us, is a place of
glory. It is the ultimate mountain of his holiness, for
more than anywhere else it reveals the character of
God, the loving Saviour.

Something of this is in his mind, for the next thing
we find Jesus saying concerns what is now his consistent theme: 'The Son of Man is going to be betrayed
into human hands, and they will kill him, and on
the third day he will be raised' (Matthew 17.23; see
also 26.45).

Three times he has told them now. He might have
hoped that by now there might be the beginnings of
acceptance, of perception. After all there is no hint
that he has told them with any sense of anxiety. There
is a confidence about the Jesus of Caesarea Philippi, a
serenity about the Jesus of the transfiguration, a
fidelity about the Jesus who cures the epileptic. It is
only Luke who actually says that at this point Jesus
'set his face to go to Jerusalem' (Luke 9.51), but in
fact in this whole sequence of events and predictions
you can see Jesus turning towards Jerusalem to suffer
and to die and trying to turn his disciples that way
too. We are bidden to follow, so that we may see his
lordship, his glory and his holiness revealed on the
Mount of Olives and on Golgotha Hill.

The transfiguration has been one instance of a
kind of anticipated glory, a glimpse of the risen,
ascended Lord. The prediction of the passion that
goes on to say that 'on the third day he will be raised'
is another. And there is just one hill-top experience

more before the picture will be completed. Once again it is the Mount of Olives. Luke tells how Jesus

> *led them out as far as Bethany, and, lifting up his hands, he blessed them. While he was blessing them, he withdrew from them and was carried up into heaven.*
>
> Luke 24.50–52

The twentieth-century Welsh poet, Saunders Lewis, captures in a delightful way the return of the Son to the Father. He calls his poem 'Ascension Thursday', but for me it speaks too of the transfiguration. 'Come and see the Father kissing the Son in the white dew' sums up wonderfully the experience on the mountain of his holiness.

> *What's on this May morning in the hills?*
> *Look at them, at the gold of the broom and laburnum*
> *And the bright surplice on the shoulders of the thorn*
> *And the intent emerald of the grass and the still calves;*
>
> *See the candlestick of the chestnut tree alight,*
> *The groves kneeling and the mute birch a nun,*
> *The cuckoo's two-notes over the shining hush of*
> *   the brook*
> *And the form of the mist bending from the censer*
> *   of the meadows:*
>
> *Come out, you men, from the council houses before*
> *The rabbits scamper, come with the weasel to see*
> *The elevation of the unblemished host*
> *And the Father kissing the Son in the white dew.*
>
> Siwan a Cherddi Eraill

SIX

Oil of Gladness

❧ ❧

The Fifth Week of Lent

In the fifth week of Lent, there is a change of mood. All the way from Ash Wednesday, there has been a movement towards the cross, but now we enter Passiontide. It's something of an oddity, for at a certain level nothing changes, and there is still a week to go before the events of Palm Sunday and beyond. But it is a week to prepare with a greater intensity for what lies beyond. It has stories of its own, not least, as Matthew, Mark and John tell it, the account of the anointing at Bethany. It is a fascinating story, not only because the evangelists place it at different points in the unfolding drama, but because they alter it in quite fundamental ways and certainly have different truths to convey through the telling of it. But at its heart, in every account, is an anointing. To enter Passiontide reflecting on anointing has a lot to be said for it. It is a sign rich in meaning, one that the Church has begun to recover, not least at this time of the year.

Joanna Anderson, who was Warden of the Iona Community from 1992 to 1995, has written movingly of the place of anointing in the Passiontide liturgy of the community there during those three years.

A special place was given to anointing during our week long programme of Experiencing Easter. The Wednesday

of Holy Week was taken as the day when our evening
worship would focus on the anointing of Jesus by a
woman. The remembering of the woman's loving touch,
her sacrificial giving and preparation of Jesus' body for
the grave are all elements called to mind in the service.
The service would be led by one or two women, lay or
ordained, and the anointing was the work of women.

The congregation seated throughout the ancient
abbey church heard readings and joined in prayer and
song focussed on the loving touch of God in creation
and in human life, and on the ways in which humanity avoids touch or abuses touch, even the loving touch
of God. Following prayers of confession, this invitation
was issued

It was a woman's touch,
a woman's gift of love poured out.
It was a woman's prophetic sign,
anointing him, preparing him
for the day of his burial.
It was an outrageous waste,
an extravagantly generous outpouring of precious
    perfume,
and the scent of her outrageous gesture filled the
    whole house.
In memory of her
and mindful of God's prodigal love,
we invite you this evening
to receive on the palm of your hands
the cross – the sign of God's love.

Anointing with Oil in Christian Worship

There is an echo of the Ash Wednesday liturgy. Rather differently, it reads, 'I invite you to receive on your head in ash the sign of the cross, the symbol of our salvation' (*Lent, Holy Week, Easter*).

Passiontide can be a very masculine sort of time. The key players in the biblical story – as well as the Lord himself, apostles and soldiers and priests and rulers and thieves – are the men, or so it seems, except for the silent women at the foot of the cross when the sky turned dark. Yet there is this crucial powerful story of the woman who took the perfumed oil and anointed the Lord.

John tells it, in chapter 12 of his Gospel, as happening six days before the Passover. The woman is identified – it is Mary, the sister of Martha and Lazarus – and it happens at supper time in their home at Bethany.

> *Mary took a pound of costly perfume made of pure nard, anointed Jesus' feet, and wiped them with her hair. The house was filled with the fragrance of the perfume. But Judas Iscariot, one of his disciples (the one who was about to betray him), said, 'Why was this perfume not sold for three hundred denarii and the money given to the poor?' . . . Jesus said, 'Leave her alone. She bought it so that she might keep it for the day of my burial. You always have the poor with you, but you do not always have me.'*
>
> John 12.3–8

All this happens just a few days before Jesus will be on his knees with the bowl of water and the towel to

wash the disciples' feet. But Mary gets there first in a
role that is neither passive nor recipient, but active
and in control.

That, of course, is how John tells it. And Luke is
not dissimilar, though he places the story much earlier in the ministry of Jesus, and the woman is not
Mary, but an unnamed woman who was a sinner, and
the house is not that of Lazarus, but of Simon the
Leper. Christopher Evans writes of the Lucan
account:

*A highly affecting scene. As Jesus reclines at the table
the woman stands behind him in such a way as to be
over against his feet. On these she lets drop tears, and
in order to turn this into a foot-washing uses her hair,
perhaps let down for the purpose, as a towel to wipe
them off. She then continues kissing the feet, though
at one point anointing them with oil brought for the
purpose.*

Saint Luke

Jesus himself spells out the meaning of her action a
little later in dialogue with his host:

*You gave me no water for my feet, but she has bathed
my feet with her tears and dried them with her hair.
You gave me no kiss, but from the time I came in she
has not stopped kissing my feet. You did not anoint my
head with oil, but she has anointed my feet with ointment. Therefore, I tell you, her sins, which were many,
have been forgiven; hence she has shown great love.*

Luke 7.44-47

For Luke the meaning is more in what it says of extravagant, impulsive, even over the top, generosity that points perhaps to an extravagant, impulsive, even an over the top kind of generous God who is profligate with his grace.

For John it is the anointing that precedes burial, for there was to be no time for that when they took him down from the cross, and he had come out of the tomb before they got there with their oils very early on the Sunday morning – too late. But this anointing anticipated his burial and was, like every anointing, a medicine of healing.

But for Matthew and for Mark, who place the story at the very heart of Holy Week after the Palm Sunday entry, it's different again. For it is his head that the woman anoints. It is a kind of coronation of the messiah before the coronation procession enters the holy city. 'Messiah', they called him, literally 'the Anointed One of God', and here is the anointing – and the crown will follow soon enough, pressed on by a high priest, though it be a crown of thorns.

Whether a sign of an extravagant God of love, or of the grave from which Christ will burst out in the new life of the resurrection, or of the Anointed One who is both priest and king, the anointing renews the Lord, refreshes him, strengthens him; and it is a woman's work.

That most familiar of psalms, Psalm 23, gives a picture of a God who anoints his faithful ones:

You prepare a table before me
in the presence of my enemies;

> *you anoint my head with oil;*
> *my cup overflows.*

Psalm 23.5

Another psalm, 45, speaks of the 'oil of gladness':

> *Your throne, O God, endures for ever and ever.*
> *Your royal sceptre is a sceptre of equity;*
> *you love righteousness and hate wickedness.*
> *Therefore God, your God, has anointed you*
> *with the oil of gladness beyond your companions.*

Psalm 45.6–7

For many clergy, and for an increasing number of laity, one of the powerful moments of Passiontide is when the Bishop invites them to join him, usually in his cathedral on Maundy Thursday morning, for a liturgy traditionally called the Mass of the Chrism. It is an entirely different service from the liturgy of the evening, the Eucharist of the Last Supper, and its focus is quite elsewhere. The Bishop summons his priests and deacons to meet with him to renew their ordination vows before leading their congregations through the hours of the passion, but also to bless the holy oils – the oil used to make the sign of the cross before baptism, the oil used for the healing of the sick and the strengthening of the dying, the oil of chrism, standing for the anointing of the Holy Spirit, following baptism or confirmation or ordination. It used to be an odd occasion, to be honest, for the clergy came and the oils were blessed, but then through the year the oils went almost unused.

Those of us who are older in the Christian faith

belong to the dry generation. We were not anointed at our baptism or our confirmation. I was not anointed when I was ordained a priest, though I have been anointed since at the beginning of a new ministry and it was a moment of great spiritual intensity. It was not my head that was anointed – the only kingship coming my way is to be part of the royal family of the Church of which we are all members. Nor was it my feet that were anointed – though washing feet and having feet washed has become important to me on Maundy Thursday. It is as powerful a sacramental act as any I know. No, it was my hands that were anointed, just as it is the hands of new priests that are sometimes anointed now at ordinations. The hands that bless, that absolve, that touch, that write, that receive; they are anointed by the one who empowers and heals, gives his Spirit and moistens what has become dry.

In the thirteenth century, Archbishop Stephen Langton wrote a great hymn to the Holy Spirit:

> *Heal our wounds; our strength renew;*
> *on our dryness pour thy dew;*
> > *wash the stains of guilt away;*
> *bend the stubborn heart and will;*
> *melt the frozen, warm the chill . . .*
> > 'Come, thou Holy Spirit, Come', *Common Praise*

Those who have translated it have tried to capture the sense of the renewal that comes when dryness, aridity, gives way to the moistness that comes with the anointing of the Spirit, like the warmth of the spring rains. For many will testify that the restoration of anointing has brought to them a wonderful new sense of the God who touches lives with love and joy, forgiveness and power.

It needs to be like that for those who come for baptism and confirmation, as many will in churches and cathedrals at Easter, especially perhaps in that powerful liturgy celebrated in the night of Easter Eve or as dawn breaks next morning, but indeed for all who are baptized or confirmed in any context. The baptism liturgy needs to proclaim to them a wonderful, surprising, gracious God, the one who inspired the woman to expend money on a precious perfume and to cry big tears and wipe them away with her hair.

I was once baptizing and came to the moment to anoint the child. The oil was brought to me in a little container an inch in diameter. Inside was a piece of almost dried up cotton wool with just a hint of oil. I wondered what shrivelled up mean-minded god that proclaimed. A god who made you sad. But I once saw an amazing video of the Easter night liturgy in a downtown American parish – *This is the Night* it was called. The moment came for the anointing of the newly baptized. The ministers approached each candidate with a great jug of oil and poured it over the head of each and massaged it in a bit like hair shampoo. What kind of generous over the top embracing God did that proclaim? The God who makes you glad.

Passiontide arrives with its invitation to let its words and silences and ceremonies be like a washing and an anointing – refreshing us, making us more alive; aridity giving way to moistness, recovering our faith and trust in the one who was anointed for a kingdom with a crown of thorns, for a grave that could not hold him and for a love that proved stronger than death. The invitation is to be like the woman who loved him almost too much, but only because from him she had received the love that took her sins away.

Janet Morley puts these words on to the lips of Jesus as she reflects on Mark's account of the woman who anointed the Lord:

> In the midst of the company I sat alone,
> and the hand of death took hold of me;
> I was cold with secrecy,
> and my God was far away.
>
> For this fear did my mother conceive me,
> and to seek this pain did I come forth?
> Did her womb nourish me for the dust,
> or her breasts, for me to drink bitterness . . .
>
> I was desolate, and she came to me;
> when there was neither hope nor help for pain
> she was at my side;
> in the shadow of the grave she has restored me.
>
> My cup was spilling with betrayal,
> but she has filled it with wine;
> my face was wet with fear,
> but she has anointed me with oil,

and my hair is damp with myrrh.
The scent of her love surrounds me;
it is more than I can bear.

She has touched me with authority;
in her hands I find strength.
For she acts on behalf of the broken,
and her silence is the voice of the unheard.
Though many murmur against her, I will praise her;
and in the name of the unremembered,
I will remember her.

Janet Morley, All Desires Known

Is she writing only of the woman who anointed the Lord? Or is she finding, in the woman with her ointment and her tears, a clue to the character of God?

SEVEN

Tree of Glory

❧☙

Holy Week

During Passiontide the Eucharist often includes this striking sentence:

> *The tree of shame became the tree of glory;*
> *and where life was lost, there life has been restored.*
>
> Passiontide Short Preface, *Common Worship*

This is not scripture, but an ancient liturgical text that we hear as part of the preface of the Eucharistic Prayer during the season of the Passion. 'The tree of glory' – it is a striking phrase. But there is quite a careful path to tread if we are to get from the cruel pain of a rough-hewn cross and a criminal's death to a tree of glory where life has been restored.

The task begins with a search in the scriptures. Almost as fundamental to the scriptures as the water, with which Genesis begins, is the tree that grows near it. The work of creation is only just being completed, when

> *the LORD God planted a garden in Eden, in the east;*
> *and there he put the man whom he had formed. Out*
> *of the ground the LORD God made to grow every tree*
> *that is pleasant to the sight and good for food, the tree*
> *of life also in the midst of the garden, and the tree of*
> *the knowledge of good and evil.*
>
> Genesis 2.8–9

This paradise scene is soon destroyed when the man, the woman and the serpent conspire in an act of rebellion – the taking and eating of the forbidden fruit described in Genesis 3 – that drives them out of the garden, fallen from grace. There is much to explore in that powerful myth, but for our immediate purposes we need to hold on to just this one thing. There is a green tree, living, life-giving in a sense, and yet it becomes for them, because of their folly, a sign of death and destruction. The tree of glory becomes the tree of shame and eternal life is lost to the sons and daughters of Adam.

From that starting point, the scriptures take us through the millennia of human life, through generations with their sagas and their histories, their prophetic utterances, their songs and their laments, until an Old Covenant, between God and his people, gives way to a New. There is a gospel, there is a Church, and the scriptures end – it is in the very last chapter of the Revelation to John – once again with water, but also with the tree of life.

> *Then the angel showed me the river of the water of life, bright as crystal, flowing from the throne of God and of the Lamb through the middle of the street of the city. On either side of the river is the tree of life, with its twelve kinds of fruit, producing its fruit each month; and the leaves of the tree are for the healing of the nations.*
>
> Revelation 22.1–2

Something significant has happened, for life is apparently no longer lost. Life has been restored. The tree is bearing fruit and it is for the healing of the nations.

The answer lies somewhere in the cross of Christ. It is in the cross that this reversal comes about. Holy Week begins with trees as people cut down their branches to strew them in the path of the king who comes into his holy city in search of his crown of thorns. But it is indeed a crown of thorns, and there is nothing life-giving about that, any more than there is about the wood he is compelled to carry. It is difficult to believe the wood that they turned into a cross would be anything but long dead and death-giving.

Jesus himself, with the heavy cross loaded on his back, turns to the women of Jerusalem who followed him wailing on the road to Golgotha:

> *Daughters of Jerusalem, do not weep for me, but weep for yourselves and for your children. For the days are surely coming when they will say, 'Blessed are the barren, and the wombs that never bore, and the breasts that never nursed' . . . For if they do this when the wood is green, what will happen when it is dry?*
>
> Luke 23.28–31

Jesus knew about wood. It is one of the ironies of the Gospels that he was, as they believed, the carpenter's son; working with wood was his trade. He knew about wood as he struggled to Golgotha with the dead weight of the dead tree on his back. But there is just a hint here, in his words to the women, that the cross is life-giving, for the wood, he says, is green.

But let me take you back for a moment into the old Hebrew scriptures in search of words that could throw light upon how the tree of shame might become the tree of glory. We need to go back to Job, the long-sufferer, and to his engagement with where God might be in the suffering. Here we find these words:

> For there is hope for a tree,
>> if it is cut down, that it will sprout again,
>> and that its shoots will not cease.
> Though its root grows old in the earth,
>> and its stump dies in the ground,
> yet at the scent of water it will bud
>> and put forth branches like a young plant.
>
> Job 14.7–9

And then Job makes a depressing comparison. That may be true for the tree, he says, but for the human race:

> Mortals die, and are laid low;
>> humans expire, and where are they?
> As waters fail from a lake,
>> and a river wastes away and dries up,
> so mortals lie down and do not rise again;
>> until the heavens are no more, they will not awake
>> or be roused out of their sleep.
> Oh that you would hide me in Sheol,
>> that you would conceal me until your wrath is past,
>> that you would appoint a set time, and remember me!
>
> Job 14.10–13

And then, with just a hint of hope, as if he is not quite convinced by his own misery, he asks:

If mortals die, will they live again?
All the days of my service I would wait
until my release should come.

Job 14.14

Here we are given in Job 14 some illumination and it comes at two levels. First of all, and perhaps more obviously, here is a passage for Easter Eve, for the Jesus who lies dead in the tomb, whose soul is taken to Sheol, as the biblical picture puts it, and waits for his release to come. But the message is not only for Easter Eve, with its hint that God can bring back to life. It is also for Good Friday with its message that the death of the tree may not be quite what it seems. There it may seem to lose its life, but it will be restored. For all that it seems to spell death, it is a source of life. At the scent of water it will bud, it will put forth branches, it will bear fruit. The cross of Christ may have seemed to those who stood at its foot like another tree that spelt banishment, disaster and shame, but through the eyes of faith it can be seen that here life was being restored; deep down in the roots there was glory.

And it is a single verse in the First Letter of Peter that makes explicit the image of the cross as a tree, when it says very simply and without any suggestion that it is saying anything very new or creative: 'He himself carried up our sins in his body to the tree' (1 Peter 2.24). It is this verse that links Genesis and Revelation and interprets all that lies between them in terms of the salvation wrought upon the cross, the tree of shame turned tree of glory, the tree of loss turned tree of life restored.

- **Tree of Glory** -

The Christian liturgical tradition has picked it up, not least in its hymnody, so that we find ourselves singing in Passiontide the words of Venantius Fortunatus, written in the sixth century:

> O Tree of beauty, Tree of light,
> O Tree with royal purple dight,
> Elect on whose triumphal breast
> Those holy limbs should find their rest!
>
> On whose dear arms, so widely flung,
> The weight of this world's ransom hung,
> The price of humankind to pay
> And spoil the spoiler of his prey.

'The royal banners forward go', *New English Hymnal*

And on Good Friday itself, *Crux fidelis*:

> Faithful Cross! above all other,
> One and only noble Tree!
> None in foliage, none in blossom,
> None in fruit thy peer may be;
> Sweetest wood and sweetest iron!
> Sweetest weight is hung on thee.

'Faithful Cross! above all other', *New English Hymnal*

This is the picture of the cross that allows John in his Revelation to see the tree of life restored and its leaves for the healing of the nations.

So how are we to approach this cross, this tree of glory? At different moments scripture bids us follow four related but distinct approaches.

The first is the call of Jesus to 'take up the cross'.

And it is important to hear that call first without the word that is sometimes added – 'daily' (to which I will return). Jesus has, in Mark's and Matthew's Gospels, two basic invitations that almost become imperatives. The first is overwhelming, but has no hint of suffering: 'Follow me' (Mark 1.17). The first disciples did indeed respond and followed him, as Christians have in every succeeding generation. But then he issues a tougher invitation, reinforcing the first, 'Take up your cross and follow me' (see Mark 8.34). And I think that the way Mark and Matthew understand the meaning of that more challenging invitation is this: 'Follow me, but know it will mean suffering, it will mean persecution; there is a cost to discipleship.' That is part of what the cross calls forth from us, a willingness to embrace a path of discipleship that is costly. It is almost impossible for me to know what that might mean for some. I do not live in a culture where being a Christian leads to persecution and even to martyrdom. Some of our young people in their schools have to make a costly stand for their faith and understand it better than older people. But even they do not really know the cost of discipleship that some face. We do well to pause for a moment to remember with thanksgiving those who in many parts of the world witness for Christ with such cost to their discipleship that 'taking up the cross' is hardly a metaphor, but very close to reality. There could be circumstances in which Christian people in the West might be called to that kind of costly discipleship. But more often we identify with that call by our prayers for others who face the time of trial, whether in Nigeria, Sudan, Pakistan or North India, in every place where being a Christian is a dangerous business.

But then there is Luke; and Luke adds to the words of Jesus 'every day' – 'take up their cross daily and follow me' (Luke 9.23). Perhaps he was writing out of a world where persecution was not so real, where the time of trial did not threaten so clearly, and discipleship was not so obviously costly. So he adds his 'daily' which gives us a different dimension. It moves the focus from persecution for the faith to things that seem 'cross-like' in our experience of life from day to day.

For even in a culture without persecution, there are experiences of suffering that are so overwhelming or painful that they are experienced as the carrying of a heavy cross through life – every day. It never leaves you, it is always a burden. It may be a kind of disability, it may be an element of personality disorder, it may be constant physical pain. And it is part of the ambivalence of life that God seems sometimes to ask people to carry a burden that feels like a cross, yet also invites them to lean on him, to allow him to bear the weight for them. We need to be very wary of expressions like 'we all have our crosses to bear', for that could be used about trifling irritations and inconveniences that don't deserve to be associated with the sufferings of Christ. But 'daily' implies a consciousness of the cross all the time, a way of living life that sees the cross in every situation. And, of course, that is what our baptismal commitment means, working out our salvation in terms of Christ's pattern of dying and living every day, so that everything, not just the things that obviously relate either to faith or to the trials of life, comes under the scrutiny of the cross.

So taking up our cross every day is subtly different from the more simple, 'Take up your cross'. Different yet again is a third approach – 'look out from the cross'. Scripture never specifically tells us to do that, but it is implicit in the call to be like Christ, to be conformed to his image and his pattern. In other words we are called to see the world, to see the Church, to see our human brothers and sisters, as Christ sees them, and as he saw them when on the cross he saw himself drawing the whole world to him. It is a very important message for Holy Week. We are not just trying to get inside the mind of Peter or Pilate, the high priest or the centurion, or Mary who anointed his feet or Mary who stood at the cross. We are trying to get into the mind of Christ, to experience, as far as our imagination will allow, what he experienced and so to be conformed to his way of breathing and living and dying. We are wanting to look with love upon the world and with yearning for its peace and the wholeness of its peoples. So to look out from the cross is always part of the Christian vocation, to try to be where Christ is, to see with his eyes, love with his love, and never more so than in Holy Week.

Finally, the call is to 'gaze upon the cross'. Not carry it, nor even look down from it, but fix one's eyes upon it and wonder at the love it represents, wonder at the life it gives, wonder at the strange hidden glory that John believed was there. 'Now the Son of Man has been glorified and God has been glorified in him. If God has been glorified in him, God will also glorify him in himself and will glorify him at once' (John 13.31–32). And the glory for John shines forth from the cross. To worship, to adore, to be silent and to be profoundly moved is the only authentic response. One of the moments in the Holy Week liturgy that touches me most deeply is to see people move through the church and into the sanctuary itself to kneel for a moment, or to stand if kneeling is too difficult, upon the pavement of the sanctuary, to pray or perhaps just to wonder at the mysterious heart of faith that in the cross – and often it is just a rough hewn piece of wood – is hidden a tree of glory, of triumph, of life restored.

I believe we are bidden to do these four things if we are to make sense of the tree of glory. We are to take up the cross, to take up the cross every day, to look out from the cross, and to gaze at the cross and, in doing all these, to ponder on the love of God.

The sense of the nobility and the triumph of the cross goes back to Paul and to John in the New Testament. Paul speaks of the folly of the cross being the wisdom of God and John of the cross as the instrument of accomplishment and of glory. Centuries on, yet more than a thousand years ago, the writer of the anonymous Anglo-Saxon poem 'The Dream of the Rood' explored the mystery of the noble tree in ways that resonate both with scripture and with our contemporary reflections.

Many years ago – the memory abides –
I was felled to the ground at the forest's edge,
Severed from my roots. Enemies seized me,
Made of me a mark of scorn for criminals to
    mount on;
Shoulder-high they carried me and set me on a hill.
Many foes made me fast there. Far off then I saw
The King of all mankind coming in great haste,
With courage keen, eager to climb me . . .
Then the young Hero – it was God almighty –
Strong and steadfast, stripped himself for battle;
He climbed up on the high gallows, constant in
    his purpose,
Mounted it in sight of many, mankind to ransom.
Horror seized me when the Hero clasped me,
But I dared not bow or bend down to earth.
Nor falter, nor fall; firm I needs must stand.
I was raised up a Rood, a royal King I bore,
The High King of Heaven: hold firm I must.
They drove dark nails through me, the dire wounds
    still show,
Cruel, gaping gashes, yet I dared not give as good.
They taunted the two of us; I was wet with teeming
    blood,
Streaming from the warrior's side when he sent
    forth his spirit.
High upon that hill helpless I suffered
Long hours of torment; I saw the Lord of hosts
Outstretched in agony; all embracing darkness
Covered with thick clouds the corpse of the
    World's Ruler;

— Tree of Glory —

The bright day was darkened by a deep shadow,
All its colours clouded; the whole creation wept,
Keened for its King's fall; Christ was on the Rood.
Yet warriors from afar eagerly came speeding
To where he hung alone. All this I beheld.

Anon., translated by Helen Gardner,
in Helen Gardner (ed.), *Faber Book of Religious Verse*

EIGHT
Garden of Delight

Easter Week

There in the garden of tears,
my heavy load he chose to bear;
his heart with sorrow was torn,
'Yet not my will but yours,' he said.

'The Servant King', *Common Praise*

Graham Kendrick's popular song 'The Servant King' attaches to the Garden of Gethsemane, where Jesus prays on Maundy Thursday night, the title 'garden of tears'. That is appropriate, though Luke tells us, not of tears, but of sweat that 'became like great drops of blood' (Luke 22.44), which is a more powerful picture. You might also describe the Garden of Eden, from which Adam and Eve are expelled, as a garden of tears, whether they be the tears of the banished man and woman or the tears of the creator whose creation has rebelled. The garden of the resurrection is also a garden of tears of grief, for Mary stands outside the tomb weeping, though later they give way to tears of joy in her reunion with the Risen Lord. It is not a biblical phrase, 'garden of tears', but it does encompass three highly significant scenes.

Similarly the 'garden of delight' is not a phrase from scripture, but carries rich meaning. We find it in one of the Eucharistic Prayers of *Common Worship*, but its origins lie in the seventh-century Liturgy of St Basil:

> *You fashioned us in your image*
> *and placed us in the garden of your delight.*
>
> Eucharistic Prayer F, *Common Worship*

You can picture the garden of Eden, newly created by God, as a source of divine delight. But you can imagine the delight also of Mary Magdalene when she encounters the Risen Lord in the garden of the resurrection and perhaps even the delight of the Father himself looking upon the Son, who bears the scars, reversing the misfortune of Adam and re-opening the garden of paradise to all believers. Gardens of tears and gardens of delight both have their place in the story of salvation.

Alongside the river and the tree that feature in the opening chapters of Genesis and reappear in the final chapter of Revelation, there is the garden, though in this case the New Testament equivalent to the Genesis passage is not in Revelation (which ends in a city), but in the Gospel accounts of the resurrection. It is in that resurrection story that there is the supreme divine reversal that restores life and relationship.

> *The LORD God planted a garden in Eden, in the east; and there he put the man whom he had formed. Out of the ground the LORD God made to grow every tree that is pleasant to the sight and good for food, the tree of life also in the midst of the garden, and the tree of the knowledge of good and evil.*
>
> Genesis 2.8–9

This is indeed a garden of delight. As Genesis pictures it, God takes pleasure in the act of creation. Myth it may be, but myth full of truth when it reveals a creator who loves his world into being and takes real delight in the realization that it is 'very good'. He makes a garden – the garden of Eden – and into it he puts the man he has made, Adam, the one who is in his image, the one with whom he yearns for relationship. Yet in this garden of delight, God has also put the tree that will undo the relationship and bring about the alienation of Adam from his creator. Perhaps for humankind to come of age it had to be. The Christian tradition struggles somewhat with the concept of the Fall. It seems a disaster, and yet, in a strange way, it seems it had to be. In the Exsultet, the ancient song that greets the resurrection in the liturgy of Easter night, the deacon sings

> *O happy fault, O necessary sin of Adam,*
> *which gained for us so great a redeemer.*
>
> The Sunday Missal

Necessary or not, the truth is that sin comes into the story and into the world through the disobedience of Adam and Eve, when they eat the forbidden fruit. The garden loses its delight and becomes instead a place of tears as they are driven out of it:

> *The LORD God sent him forth from the garden of Eden, to till the ground from which he was taken. He drove out the man; and at the east of the garden of Eden he placed the cherubim, and a sword*

flaming and turning to guard the way to the tree of life.

Genesis 3.23–24

Hilary Greenwood, in a simple yet moving hymn of the last century, writes:

Walking in a garden
At the close of day,
Adam tried to hide him
When he heard God say:
'Why are you so frightened,
Why are you afraid?
You have brought the winter in,
Made the flowers fade.'

'Walking in a garden', *New English Hymnal*

The cold winter in the garden is the alienation of the human race, which becomes a race condemned. Genesis sees it as condemnation to pain, to toil, to sweat and ultimately to death – 'you are dust, and to dust you shall return' (Genesis 3.19). What a contrast with the garden of innocence, delight, pleasure and friendship with God. As Paul sees it, through the disobedience of the one man, death came into the world (1 Corinthians 15.21) and, worse than that, by that one man's disobedience, many were made sinners (Romans 5.19). It is not only Adam who is banished from the garden, but the whole human race, living tantalizingly in sight of Eden, but excluded from it. The gate has been closed and humankind expelled.

There is wisdom in Elizabeth Jennings' poem, 'Touch'. In the garden of the resurrection, the Lord will say 'Touch me not till I have ascended', but here, thinking of the garden of creation, she observes:

Touch. How much it starts and how much it ends.
Each sacrament demands it and all love,
Whether of passion or the play of friends,

Asks for its use. God started this world of
Shape and substance. The whole universe
Stirred by his touching it at every move.

Eden – the potent tale of our reverse,
Was darkened by the picking of a fruit
When touch was disobedient. Its curse

Spoilt touch and yet it also somehow brought
God-Man to us and put him at our will.
Touch can demonstrate an arcane thought

And love surrenders when its power goes still.

Elizabeth Jennings, In the Meantime

The garden has lost its delight. But this 'potent tale of our reverse' is itself capable of reverse when Jesus comes to open the gate that has barred the entry of humankind. Before that he comes into that other garden, Gethsemane, where he prays to the Father that, if it is possible, the cup may pass him by.

Walking in a garden
Where the Lord had gone,
Three of the disciples,
Peter, James, and John . . .

Hilary Greenwood's hymn continues:

> *They were very weary,*
> *Could not keep awake,*
> *While the Lord was kneeling there,*
> *Praying for their sake.*

Jesus has come from the supper in the upper room into the garden. There he prays to the Father as the time of his death draws near. If Adam was driven from the garden to a life of pain, toil and sweat and to the ultimate destiny of death, Jesus, the man condemned, now lives out that human vocation quite uncannily. Here in the garden is the sweat that is like great drops of blood. Soon will come the toil of the journey to Calvary with the heavy cross on his back and then the pain of the nails before the condemned man meets with death. But perhaps we should see a hint of something else, for the angels are back in the picture, no longer guarding the gates to keep the exile out, but appearing to Jesus and giving him strength (Luke 22.43), just as they did in the wilderness. In Eden evil in the guise of the serpent led the man astray. Here in Gethsemane the temptation is being resisted and evil is losing its grip. Here there is a reversal of Adam's disobedience. Here Jesus with perfect obedience prays 'Not my will but yours be done' (Luke 22.42).

Then comes the cross and after it the placing in the tomb that Joseph of Arimathea has prepared for himself. Only John tells us clearly where it was.

> *Now there was a garden in the place where he was*
> *crucified, and in the garden there was a new tomb in*

*which no one had ever been laid. And so, because it
was the Jewish day of Preparation, and the tomb was
nearby, they laid Jesus there.*

John 19.41–42

Remember in John nothing is ever without meaning.
The new tomb is in a garden. It is almost as if Eden
has been recreated. There is about to be new life, for
God is beginning again – and this time it will not all
go wrong. John V. Taylor reflects on this, on life and
death, on womb and tomb, in his poem, 'Diptych':

*He who lay curled in Mary's womb,
starting and ending in a cave,
has broken new-born from the tomb.*

*His star outshone the smothering gloom,
searching for those he came to save.
He who lay curled in Mary's womb*

*to take upon himself our doom,
and our unkindnesses forgave,
has broken new-born from the tomb.*

*Again they offered sweet perfume,
myrrh for his helpless limbs they gave,
he who lay curled in Mary's womb.*

*Swaddling allows too little room;
he that was bound from crib to grave
has broken new-born from the tomb.*

Angels again brought tidings: 'Whom
seekest thou? See, the Lord you crave,
he who lay curled in Mary's womb,
has broken new-born from the grave.'

A Christmas Sequence

This is the moment to which our Lenten journey has been moving. It is like a new birth. The Lord comes from the tomb. It is a new beginning, a new creation. Paradise is restored. Once again the man stands in the garden of delight. God looks upon what he has made and it is very good indeed.

Paul is clear that just as the first man's disobedience was a sign of the alienation of all humankind, the obedience of this new man, seen in Gethsemane and on Golgotha, is also a sign, and much more than a sign, of a relationship restored. Indeed if the one spelt death, the other now spells life. Of course it does not remove physical death, but it promises an immortal eternal life with God. 'As all die in Adam, so all will be made alive in Christ' (1 Corinthians 15.22).

The gate of death has been opened. Where Genesis pictures the cherubim guarding the garden of Eden so that Adam and Eve may not return, now the evangelists picture the stone rolled back and the tomb empty, guarded by angels whose message is, not to keep out, but to invite the disciples in. The invitation is not into the dark tomb itself (though that has to be explored by some of them), but into a renewed utterly different relationship with the risen Lord. Mark's news of the resurrection is told with a wonderful simplicity:

*Very early on the first day of the week, when the sun
had risen, they went to the tomb. They had been saying to one another, 'Who will roll away the stone for
us from the entrance to the tomb?' When they looked
up, they saw that the stone, which was very large, had
already been rolled back. As they entered the tomb,
they saw a young man, dressed in a white robe, sitting
on the right side; and they were alarmed. But he said
to them, 'Do not be alarmed; you are looking for Jesus
of Nazareth, who was crucified. He has been raised;
he is not here. Look, there is the place they laid him.
But go, tell his disciples and Peter that he is going
ahead of you to Galilee; there you will see him, just as
he told you'.*

Mark 16.2–7

At first fear overcame them. It was the garden of ter-
ror, but only until they had time to assimilate the
truth. Then it became indeed the garden of delight.
The gate was now open and the angel was beckoning
them in.

Drawn back into Eden, so to speak, those first disciples are soon encountering the one who has made
it all possible, this new man, who bears the scars of
the passion, but has glory written all over his body.
Scripture captures the sheer joy of that encounter in
the meeting of Mary Magdalene with her Lord. And
if we need any further reminder that this is the story
of a garden, about a relationship restored and a return
from exile, John provides a subtle hint. 'Supposing
him to be the gardener,' John writes (John 20.15),

and, of course, in a way he is. For he has made the garden beautiful again and invited them in.

Hilary Greenwood's Easter hymn ends like this:

Walking in a garden
at the break of day,
Mary asked the gardener
where the body lay;
but he turned towards her,
smiled at her and said:
'Mary, spring is here to stay,
only death is dead.'

The way the Christian tradition has envisaged Mary, she is a passionate loving utterly devoted follower of the Lord. Her weeping outside the tomb in gospel accounts that nearly always play down emotion is striking. And so we can picture something not unlike ecstasy, sheer delight, in her recognition of her Lord. There are passages in that unexpected love poem of the Old Testament, the Song of Solomon, that, though they were written for another context, seem to resonate with the scene in the garden and capture the ecstatic joy of Easter:

My beloved speaks and says to me:
'Arise, my love, my fair one,
    and come away;
for now the winter is past,
    the rain is over and gone.
The flowers appear on the earth;
    the time of singing has come . . .'

I will rise now and go about the city,
  in the streets and in the squares;
I will seek him whom my soul loves.
  I sought him, but found him not.
The sentinels found me,
  as they went about the city.
'Have you seen him whom my soul loves?'
Scarcely had I passed them,
  when I found him whom my soul loves.
I held him, and would not let him go . . .

Awake, O north wind,
  and come, O south wind!
Blow upon my garden
  that its fragrance may be wafted abroad.
let my beloved come to his garden,
  and eat its choicest fruits.
I come to my garden, my sister, my bride;
  I gather my myrrh with my spice,
  I eat my honeycomb with my honey,
  I drink my wine with my milk.
Eat, friends, drink,
  and be drunk with love.

Song of Solomon 2.10–12; 3.2–4; 4.16–5.1

Here are words to wonder at as we superimpose them
on the Easter story – myrrh for the one to whom the
wise men gave it at his birth, spices that the women
bring to the tomb, milk and honey for the one who
has led his people through the waters of death into
the promised land, wine for the one who would not
drink it again until he drank it new in the kingdom,
and the garden of delight itself.

Yet one line stands out as inappropriate, at least at first – 'I held him and would not let him go.' How do we set that against the familiar words of Jesus to Mary Magdalene, the moment captured in so many paintings – 'Do not hold on to me', 'touch me not' as the King James Bible puts it (John 20.17)? Touch is for Mary the natural response, as it would be for most people finding alive a dear friend whom they had thought dead and gone. To touch, to embrace, to kiss seems utterly natural. And, as Elizabeth Jennings has said,

> Touch. How much it starts and how much ends.
> Each sacrament demands it and all love,
> Whether of passion or the play of friends,
> Asks for its use.

Yet Mary meets the forbidding 'Touch me not'. It is such a powerful imperative that we can lose sight of the fact that it is only half the sentence. What Jesus says to Mary is 'Do not hold on to me, because I have not yet ascended to the Father'. In John's understanding of the mystery of Christ's death, resurrection and ascension, the going to the Father is part of the Easter Day experience itself. Mary catches Jesus in a kind of transitional state – he has burst the tomb, but he is even at that very moment experiencing the completion of this process of glorification. He is, as he instructs her to tell the disciples, 'ascending to my Father and your Father, to my God and your God' (John 20.17). This is very different from Luke's account, with its picture of the ascending Christ on

the Mount of Olives forty days on. As John under-
stands it, only a little time later the process is completed – Jesus is the risen, ascended, glorified one
who can stand among his disciples on Easter Day
evening, say 'Peace be with you' and breathe on them
the Holy Spirit.

The forbidding 'Touch me not' is only a message
for a particular moment, whether because for Jesus a
process is incomplete or because Mary needs to be
stopped in her tracks just for long enough to understand that this Lord, whom her soul loves, has been
changed. She must not hold on to him as he was; if
she is to embrace him, she must embrace the exalted
Lord he has now become. 'Touch me not' is only for
a while, and, yes, touch is demanded in all love and
in every sacrament. So it is that, only a week later,
Thomas is being invited to stretch out his hands to
touch – 'Put your finger here and see my hands.
Reach out your hand and put it in my side. Do not
doubt but believe' (John 20.27). In the Easter stories
we also see the Lord taking bread and breaking it at
Emmaus with two of his friends, and giving bread
and fish to the disciples on the lakeside. 'Each
sacrament demands it.'

In the sharing of the sacraments and in the touch
of human love, we find the life-giving love of the living Lord renewing our souls and bodies. 'Touch me
not' is only for the time it takes us to enter into the
mystery of resurrection and recognize the Risen Lord
for what, by the grace of God, he has become. Once
we have understood that, we can hold him and not let

him go, and live with the confidence that he will hold on to us and not let us go, through all the experiences through which he has gone before us, even death itself. From that confidence will come the loosening of the tongue that will not only whisper in the heart 'Alleluia, the Lord is risen,' but will proclaim aloud to a world that is searching for signs of the kingdom, 'He is risen indeed, alleluia.'

Julia Esquivel, reflecting on Isaiah 55 in relation to the resurrection, captures the sense of the garden of paradise restored and the kingdom of God thrown open, when she writes in 'Threatened with Resurrection':

> *When the hour comes,*
> *you shall change my desert into a waterfall,*
> *you shall anoint my head with fresh oil*
> *and your strength shall overcome my weakness.*
> *You shall guide my feet into your footsteps*
> *and I will walk the narrow path*
> *that leads to your house.*
>
> *You shall tell me when*
> *and where*
> *I will walk your path*
> *totally bathed in joy.*
> *In the meantime,*
> *I ask you, Lord, you who awaken*
> *in the most intimate place in my soul*
> *the Feast of Life!*
> *That of the Empty Tomb!*
> *That of the Victorious Cross!*

Let your voice mistaken as the Gardener's
awaken my hearing every morning
with news that's always fresh:
'Go and tell my brothers
that I have overcome death,
that there is a place for everyone

there where the New Nation is built.
There,
where neither earth, love or joy
can be bought or sold,
where wine and milk
are shared without money and without price.'

In Janet Morley (ed.), *Bread of Tomorrow*

References

Alves, Rubem, 'Brazilian prayer' in Janet Morley (ed.), *Bread of Tomorrow*. SPCK/Christian Aid 1992.

Anointing with Oil in Christian Worship. Norwich Diocesan Liturgical Committee 1996.

Anonymous, 'Dream of the Rood', trans. Helen Gardner, in Helen Gardner (ed.), *The Faber Book of Religious Verse*. Faber 1972.

Burgess, Ruth, 'Prayer' in Janet Morley (ed.), *Bread of Tomorrow*. SPCK/Christian Aid 1992.

Common Praise. Canterbury Press 2000.

Common Worship: Services and Prayers for the Church of England. Church House Publishing 2000.

Coughlan, Peter, Jasper, Ronald, and Rodrigues, Teresa (eds), *A Christian's Prayer Book*. Geoffrey Chapman 1973.

Eliot, T. S. 'Choruses from the Rock' (*Collected Poems 1909–1962*. Faber 1974).

Esquival, Julia, 'Threatened with Resurrection' in Janet Morley (ed.), *Bread of Tomorrow*. SPCK/Christian Aid 1992.

Evans, Christopher, *Saint Luke*. SCM Press 1990.

Gardner, Helen (ed.), *The Faber Book of Religious Verse*. Faber 1972.

Jennings, Elizabeth, *Growing Points*. Carcanet 1975.

Jennings, Elizabeth, *In the Meantime*. Carcanet 1996.

Jennings, Elizabeth, *The New Collected Poems*. Carcanet 2002.

Lent, Holy Week, Easter. Church House Publishing/Cambridge University Press/SPCK 1986.

Lewin, Ann, *Candles and Kingfishers*. Methodist Publishing House 1993.

Lewis, Saunders, 'Ascension Thursday' (*Siwan a Cherddi Eraill*, Llyfrau'r Dryw 1956; reproduced in *The Oxford Book of Welsh Verse in English*, Oxford University Press 1977).

Milner-White, Eric, *My God, My Glory*. SPCK 1954.

Morley, Janet, *All Desires Known*. SPCK 1992.

Morley, Janet (ed.), *Bread of Tomorrow*. SPCK/Christian Aid 1992.

New English Hymnal. Canterbury Press 1986.

Schweizer, Eduard, *The Good News According to Mark*. SPCK 1971.

The Sunday Missal. Collins 1975.

Taylor, John V., *A Christmas Sequence and Other Poems*. Amate Press 1989.

Teilhard de Chardin, Pierre, *Hymn of the Universe*. Collins 1965.

Underhill, Evelyn, 'Corpus Christi' in Peter Coughlan and others (eds), *A Christian's Prayer Book*. Geoffrey Chapman 1973.

Acknowledgements

The author and publisher gratefully acknowledge permission to reproduce copyright material. Every effort has been made to trace and acknowledge copyright holders. The publisher apologizes for any errors or omissions that may remain and, if notified, will ensure that full acknowledgement is made in a subsequent edition of this book.

Extracts (marked AV) from the Authorized Version of the Bible (King James Bible), the rights in which are vested in the Crown, are reproduced by permission of the Crown's Patentee, Cambridge University Press.

All other scripture quotations are from the New Revised Standard Version of the Bible, copyright © 1946, 1952 and 1971 by the Division of Christian Education of the National Council of the Churches of Christ in the USA. Used by permission. All rights reserved.

Extracts from *Common Worship: Services and Prayers for the Church of England*, published by Church House Publishing, and *Lent, Holy Week, Easter* (on p. 62), published by SPCK, Cambridge University Press and Church House Publishing, are reproduced by permission of The Archbishops' Council.

The lines from 'Choruses from the Rock' (on p. 2) from *Collected Poems 1909–1962* by T. S. Eliot are reproduced by permission of Faber and Faber Ltd.

— **Acknowledgements** —

The prayers by Ruth Burgess (on p. 4), Rubem Alves (on p. 44) and Julia Esquivel (on p. 95) in *Bread of Tomorrow* are reproduced by permission of SPCK.

The three poems, 'Holy Communion' (on p. 15), 'Christ on the Cross' (on p. 26) and 'Touch' (on pp. 86 and 93) from *The New Collected Poems* of Elizabeth Jennings, published by Carcanet, are reproduced by permission of David Higham Associates Ltd.

The poem 'Corpus Christi' (on p. 22) by Evelyn Underhill in *A Christian's Prayer Book*, published by Geoffrey Chapman, is reproduced by permission of Continuum International Publishing Ltd.

The prayer 'Fountain of Life' (on p. 34) and the lines from 'The Lord's Supper' (on p. 46) from *My God, My Glory* by Eric Milner-White, published by SPCK, are reproduced by permission of the Friends of York Minster.

The poem 'Transfiguration' from *Candles and Kingfishers* (on p. 55), published by the Methodist Publishing House, is reproduced by permission of Ann Lewin.

The poem 'Ascension Thursday' (on p. 59) by Saunders Lewis from *Siwan a Cherddi Eraill* is reproduced by permission of Dinefwr Press, Llandybie, Carmarthenshire.

The extract from *Anointing with Oil in Christian Worship* (on p. 60), published by the Norwich Diocesan Liturgical Committee, is reproduced by permission of Joanna Anderson.

The poem 'In the midst of the company' (on pp. 68–9) by Janet Morley in *All Desires Known* is reproduced by permission of SPCK.

— Acknowledgements —

The lines from the translation by Helen Gardner of 'The Dream of the Rood' (on p. 80) from *The Faber Book of Religious Verse* is reproduced by permission of the executors of the estate of the late Helen Gardner.

The lines from the 'The Servant King' by Graham Kendrick (on p. 82) are copyright © 1986 Kingsway's Thank You Music, PO Box 75, Eastbourne, East Sussex BN23 6NW, and is reproduced by kind permission of Kingsway's Thank You Music.

The hymn 'Walking in the Garden' (on pp. 85, 86 and 91) by Hilary Greenwood is reproduced by permission of The Society of the Sacred Mission.

The poem 'Diptych' (on p. 88) from *A Christmas Sequence* by John V. Taylor, published by Amate Press, is reproduced by permission of Peggy Taylor.